ERIC GILL:
Twentieth Century
Book Designer

Revised Edition

by

Elizabeth A. Brady

The Scarecrow Press, Inc.
Metuchen, N. J.   1974

Library of Congress Cataloging in Publication Data

Brady, Elizabeth A   1914-
    Eric Gill, twentieth century book designer.

    Bibliography: p.
    1. Gill, Eric, 1882-1940.
Z232.G47B7   1974   686.2'24 [B] 73-18453
ISBN 0-8108-0640-1

Copyright 1974 by Elizabeth A. Brady

TABLE OF CONTENTS

The author wishes to thank Cassell & Co., Ltd.,
J. M. Dent & Sons, Ltd., and Faber and Faber for
permission to reproduce illustrations from their
publications.

List of Illustrations

CHAPTER 1

ERIC GILL: A BOOK DESIGNER?

Printing, the major means by which ideas are reproduced visually, uses graphic symbols, arranging them so
that the space around and within them becomes an integral
part of the page design.   When viewed as art, printing becomes the vital result of a synthesis of knowledge, patience,
skill, and a deep sense of beauty.   Print adds a new di-
mension to the pages of books.   As a tool to understanding,
it becomes a transparent medium between the words of the
writer and the mind of the reader.

In the twentieth century printing assumes the character of a "Baby Blue Ox" as one attempts to analyze the
forces that produced it.   It is precisely this mechanized
giant running wild which has, of necessity, created the book
designer.   Modern fine printing, like many of the other contemporary arts, is a work of harmony: a living, corporate
whole, exquisite in all of its parts, designedly functional.
Book design has become a profession.

Today, the book as a whole adapts the graphic forms
of communication to match the character of the idea of which
it is the vehicle.   This adaptation is the work of the designer.
He must coordinate each part, using the physical and visual
forms within the whole to build his pattern.   In this century
of competitive art only a select number of printers are

1

designers of books.   Certainly only a few designers produce
good designs.

     The American Institute of Graphic Arts, with its Book
Clinics and traveling exhibits of Fifty Books of the Year, has
provided, for publishers and public alike, visual proof in
examples and has set standards of the qualities and characteristics of fine design.   The Frankfurt Book Fair is another such exhibit on an international scale, less selective
but certainly competitive, prodding for more and better designers of books.

     Eric Gill is noted as a sculptor, wood-engraver, and
author.   Although no extensive studies have been done on
that facet of his work called book design, it is the contention
of this book that he is one of the outstanding designers of
the twentieth century.

     Gill himself has provided much of the material from
which to evaluate his work as a book designer.   Considered
as a creator of fine printing, Eric Gill should embody in
his work all of the qualities of an artist, since fine printing
is an artistic production of creative intelligence and skill.
Exploring his designs critically, then, should prove both
provocative and rewarding research.

     It is axiomatic that all art must be derivative of
the past or of the present or of both.   One question to be
answered is, has Gill created honestly as an artist, using
his knowledge of the past and the present to produce "fine
books"?

     It is very possible that in the first flush of designing
Gill leaned rather heavily on patterns known to have been
satisfying in the past, even in the very far past.   In fact,
as early as 1909 Gill designed several plates for a text of
Edward Johnson, admittedly basing his work on the oldest

known letter forms--the Trajan Column (see Plate XIII).[1]

But to what extent did the traditional forces of printing influence him as a mature designer? The question takes on new color and form as the evidence is related to the times and to the philosophies of Gill.

As a man Gill appears to be a strange composite of many eras, with the Middle Ages predominating. But as an artist, does he reflect a modern element, a personal translation that allows for the creation of new forms? Are these forms actually different, a picture of the contemporary age? Are they beautiful? Herschel Levit says that "the creative artist always had that special quality which enabled him to produce a form characteristic of his time and place."[2] Gill's place as a book designer needs to be evaluated in terms of the present as well as the past.

The most feasible method of studying Gill designs may be divided into three steps, the first of which is a survey of books designed by Gill. Such a survey would be more rewarding if it considered only his mature work because it is as a mature designer that an artist reaches the height of his achievement. In Gill's case this would be books designed by him between 1928 and 1940. The second step is an analysis of the forces upon which six specific designs are based, since in these one finds the fundamental principles which were forces in Gill's work. The third step is a study of the principles underlying these same designs. While Gill expressed himself often and well his basic beliefs concerning this art are found in Typography, Sacred and Secular, Art and Civilization, and in Beauty Looks After Herself. The method includes, therefore, 1) a survey, 2) an analysis, and 3) a formula. The plates included are photocopies of original sources or of interlinear studies.

In order to evaluate Eric Gill's book designs it is
necessary to adopt certain definite cores of truth as gauges.
These definitions, while personal, have their basis in
authority, and they provide five measuring sticks for the
purpose of this work.

1. Art: Creation may be defined in the case of God
simply as an act of making something from nothing; or in the
case of an artist, as an act of making something new by
relating existing things. Etienne Gilson goes more deeply
into this problem when he says, "Art is the ability to create
a new being that nobody would ever see, either in nature
or otherwise, unless the artist caused it to exist."[3] The
quality of the thing which owes its origin directly to the
artist, not as an imitation of something seen, nor as an
idea given him by another, emerges from the totality of his
individual consciousness. Gilson sets the artist apart,
calling him "one of the creative forces of nature..." and
holding that "he gives existence to certain beings that in
nature no one else would have produced."[4] A work of art
is the new derivative of the artist. Its radiance is the
quality of its beauty.

2. Beauty is defined by St. Thomas Aquinas simply
as "That which being seen, pleases."[5] Maritain restates
this definition: "Beauty consists in knowledge and delight,"
and explains that "it makes us delighted in the very act of
knowing, a delight which overflows from the thing this act
attains."[6] The visible image is said to possess beauty
when the perception of it becomes a source of intense
pleasure. A work of art is beautiful if, as Maritain says,
"it is characterized by three marks: integrity, proportion

or consonance, and radiance or clarity. "[7] The need of the
creator to manifest externally that which he grasps intui-
tively and to manifest it in beauty is an essential quality of
the artist.

      3. Tradition is a living power in the present which
transmits the past. The very word tradition, taken etymo-
logically, means a handing down; not a handing down of
static historical images but the handing down of revitalized
forms. Tradition becomes a force only when it is used in
relation to a new problem considered in a new age that adapts
it, transforms it, and strengthens it. [8]

      4. The weight, size, thickness, and the tactile quali-
ties of a book, as well as its paper, type, illustration, and
binding, are the elements of the book in design. The design
itself is the pattern of related forms used. Considered in
its parts, design means the integration of layouts, title page,
chapter headings, and the jacket, taken in their visual se-
quence, plus the rhythm and the outward face which form
the personality of the particular book.

      5. The design of books peculiar to this age is
marked by allusive typography, function, simplicity, and a
few adventurous new forms. Book design is contemporary
only if it has a living fiber of organic growth as a basic
quality. Otherwise it would be a static thing without future;
an ephemeral illusion with no lasting quality of reality.
This definition is borne out by Walter Dorwin Teague in
an article on "Static and Dynamic Concepts of Contemporary
Book Design": "The physical format of a printed book cannot rely on static symmetry or on mere excellence of technique, or on the approved customs of the past. If it is to
be an experience of value it must first of all be simple; it

must be functionally efficient; it must display an orderly but
not a conventional adjustment of relationships among its
parts; it must have verve ... it must be a fitting vehicle...."[9]   This definition is further authenticated by
Gyorgy Kepes in his discussion of modern design when he
says that since "the laws of visual perception are condi-
tioned by visual habits of time [and since] contemporary
man's visual habit has undergone a new transformation ...
developing idioms of simplicity, forcefulness, structural
lucidity ... of clarity, precision and economy, book design
must make significant adjustment to the contemporary scene
in a dynamic visual language."[10]

The theme of an exhibit displayed by the Library of
Congress from February to May of 1956 was contained in
the title of the brochure advertising it, "Modern Art Influences on Printing Design." It delineates the place of the
modern designer in an excerpt from Paul Valery, quoted on
the verso of the cover: "The artist-printer finds himself
face to face with his task in the complicated situation of the
architect who is concerned over the harmony between the
function of his construction and its appearance.... A Book
is physically perfect when it is pleasant to read, delightful
to look at.... In final analysis all of the form must flow
from the type...."[11]

In conclusion, Herbert J. Sanborn, the compiler of
the brochure, summarizes the exhibit and expresses the
position of this work in its definition of contemporary book
design: "Modern art has introduced certain characteristics
that distinguish contemporary from traditional printing forms
and graphic design. The abstract artist felt that space was
a dynamic element and so he experimented with planes,

shapes, and volumes. In printing design these concepts
opened windows that brought new freedom. They broke with
the traditional use of uniform margins that framed the text
and illustrations. With this new freedom contemporary designers began to make asymmetrical arrangements of lines
and blocks of type or illustrations. In the new concept of
typography elements are organized on the page with a variety
of relationships.... Illustrations are not considered as dec-
orations but they are functionally used to supplement and to
clarify the text...."[12] Such a definition of contemporary
book design may prove to be a practical formula upon which
Gill designs could have been based if they are peculiarly
contemporary in spirit, that is, if they are allusive, functional, simple, vital designs including some new forms.

Notes

1. Edward Johnson. Manuscript and Inscription Letters.
    London: John Hogg, 1909. Plates 12-16.
    (Plate XIII)

2. Herschel Levit. "The Avant Garde," Graphic Forms.
    Cambridge: Harvard University Press, 1949,
    p. 73.

3. Etienne Gilson. Painting and Reality. New York:
    Pantheon Books, 1957, p. 116.

4. Ibid., p. 117.

5. St. Thomas Aquinas. P. I. Q5, Art. 4 Great Books
    Edition, p. 26.

6. Jacques Maritain. Creative Intuition in Art and Poetry.
    New York: Pantheon Books, 1953, p. 160-62.

7. Ibid., p. 163.

8. Talbot Hamlin. "The Place of Tradition in Modern

8 Eric Gill

Design," College Art Journal, XVI:307-15, Summer, 1957.

9. Walter Dorwin Teague. "Static and Dynamic Concepts," Graphic Forms. Gyorgy Kepes and others. Cambridge: Harvard University Press, 1949, p. 50.

10. Kepes. Ibid., p. 10.

11. Paul Valery. "Two Virtues of a Book," Modern Art Influences on Printing Design. Washington, D.C.: American Institute, 1956.

12. Herbert J. Sanborn. Ibid., p. 11.

CHAPTER 2

ERIC GILL:
THE TOPOGRAPHY OF A TYPOGRAPHER

If one weighs the many factors of a single human life
within the context of a panoramic quality of change, while
considering the interaction of lives one upon another and
upon that one life in particular, a certain topography evolves.
History then is seen as a multi-dimensional lifescape in
which an individual human being evidences a unique pattern
of living within the limits of his birth and death: circumstances change the pattern; sorrow or shock draws the character more finely; daring and joy fill the foreground with
bold shapes; colors--brilliant, drab, or dull--or deeply textured lines describe the day by day occurrences; harmonies,
dissonances, the slightest whisper above and beyond appear-
ances alter the design. And so a biography becomes a les-
son in human geography. [1,2]

Gill was a worker born and bred. He was a man
first, living life to the full, never a Sculptor, nor an Artist,
nor an Author in capital letters--neither in actuality nor in
desire. Such attributes always remained secondary to him.
The whole process of living a Christian life absorbed his interest, while the means of making a living as a creator of
functional, beautiful objects were tools which he employed,
enjoying their use tremendously, vitally, and with his whole
heart.

9

The world of typography was then, as now, a changing
one.   There were leading lights in typographical America and
England who looked backward toward tradition and forward to
contemporaneous expression: Dwiggins, Goudy, Rogers,
Morison, Oliver, etc.   Periodicals devoted to fine printing,
such as Ars Typographica, The Fleuron, The Dolphin, The
Colophon, Signature, were born and died.   Typographically
speaking, it was an age of struggle to throw off inhibitions,
to revert to pristine vigor, to create dynamically.

In this setting the topography of the typographer, Eric
Gill, begins.   The biography of Eric Gill could not be a quiet
unequivocal history beginning in 1882 and ending in 1940.
The thing begun has not yet finished; new approaches and
new relationships bring to it new insights.   For instance--
Gill the book designer.

But to go back to the beginning.   Eric came second into
the solid serious surroundings of a middle-class Victorian home:
second, that is, of thirteen children, and Victorian with the best
that the word implies.   Perhaps, in this the Gills were like their
Brighton neighbors.   Their home was the center of their world.
To the children the head of the house was their father, a strict
but just judge, gentle, inexorable, a lover of beauty and high
sounding words, a man of clear principles; their mother was
the beautiful, practical, sometimes harsh, often completely sub-
jective hub around which life evolved.

Yet the elder Mr. Gill was most certainly not the
typical English minister, as the mother was not the typical
Brightonite.   He combined charity and love with inflexible
principle and prudery.   During the first fifteen years of
Eric's life, Mr. Gill belonged to a small sect called the
"Countess of Huntingdon's Connection."   Faith was laid down

by him in the home like law, without too much rationality
but with the certainty of light and air.   Here too, the children were introduced to music, art and culture, as well as
to unquestioning obedience and to truth.   They were taught
fierce pride in work well done.   To them money became only
a means to an end.   In fact, the ends in life became all-
important, and poverty but an incidental good, not an evil.

Brighton itself was a hodge-podge of streets, beginning and ending nowhere in particular.   According to first
indications, the Gill family reflected this trait.   But fifteen
years after Eric's birth circumstances changed the pattern.

Their father, patriarchal head that he was, found that
he could not, either as a minister or as an individual, allow
his congregation to dictate his beliefs.   The effect of this
decision was catastrophic.   It meant that real poverty became a close family companion while Mr. Gill studied for
the ministry in the Church of England and began again in a
new parish.   It meant a certain family pride in parental integrity.   It meant exchanging the mystery and excitement of
the railroad town of Brighton for the symmetry, beauty, and
history of Chichester.   More than that, it meant embracing
austerity.   The growth-process of the young Eric during this
wintry experience was clear-cut and deep-rooted.

And this period of change brought a new acquaintance,
deep grief.   Cecily, the second sister, died.   To Eric she
had been the most dear of all his six brothers and six sisters.   He thought her completely perfect.   Irrevocable sep-
aration from her sweetness, peacefulness, and companionship
bit into the warp and woof of his adolescence.   Gill himself
says that the three succeeding years were marked by struggle
with new questions;   bitterness and rapture warred in his

young mind.   Maturity was dearly bought.

Chichester, new friends, and new work did not completely eradicate this grief.   His restlessness became inter-
active.   The boy Gill had been deeply involved in the dreams
and romances of locomotives.   But this older Gill saw the
harsh reality of railroad engineering and banished the dream.
Two new ones arose to replace it.

As a pupil enrolled in the Art School of Chichester,
Eric and his father envisioned a career for him as a painter.
The praise of the headmaster colored his dream out of all
true proportion until it came abruptly to an end.   At the Art
School Eric was a precise mechanician and a good letterer.
But he was not a good painter.   Still, something more permanent might have come of this schooling if Gill had not
fallen in love for the first time, violently, completely, and
with all of the agony and uncertainty of adolescence.   Because his teacher would and could not accept Eric's innocence
in an assumed affair and because Eric could and would not
bear the ugliness of injustice in the man he had idolized, he
left the Art School.

And then there was the second dream, running con-
currently with the first but with more serious consequences:
the dream of a career in architecture.   The lovely old city
of Chichester taught Gill to see--to see with the inner eye of
the designer.   While this dream was never brought to reality
it affected all of his later life.   The designer grew, waxed
strong and flowered.   Today we are reaping the fruit, four-
fold.

While the troubled boy haunted the churches and fields
of Chichester, daily drinking in beauty and reverence, new
and deeply moving influences were being formed.   At the

cathedral Eric made two strong friends, the Prependary and the Sacristan.   The first underwrote his career studies in architecture and the latter allowed him to court and marry his daughter.

After four years in Chichester, Gill set out for London at the age of 19.   Since the life of an architect's apprentice did not provide the means to support a wife Eric went alone, although the opposition of his family to the marriage had only made the lovers more deeply sure of their desire.

Two years of hard work, disillusionment and awakening began.   In time Eric Gill became an agnostic, a socialist, and a rebel.   The architect provided the blueprints for the worker.   The worker he found to be a mechanical stooge, and architecture itself often an unlovely copy of age-old designs which lost their meaning for a contemporary society. So, first under the tutorage of George Carter and then under Edward Johnson, lettering began to absorb the mind and time of Gill.

While he was living in Brighton the home was the center of life;   in Chichester, the city, with its communal society, was central;   living now with Edward Johnson in his rooms at Lincoln's Inn, a unanimity developed that made for a complete sharing of life.   This new experience broadened Gill in areas of thinking, public speaking, and writing as nothing else would have.   Neither Gill nor Johnson belonged at Oxford, but as guests with quarters at the Inn they became an integral part of the Oxford group.   The young Gill was becoming a thinking and a thought-provoking man.   At this time, too, Gill began to work seriously at the business of lettering, stone-cutting, and monumental masonry.

His marriage to Ethel, daughter of the Sacristan of

Chichester Cathedral, brought a certainty of desire and goal,
a peace and rapture, and a new approach to the problems of
living.   All of the experiences which had formed the man
Gill went now into the formation of a way of life to be passed
on to new lives which were his responsibility as head of the
family.

The family quickly outgrew the neighborhood in Batter-
sea.   In 1908 they moved to Ditchlings in Sussex, not alone
because it was country but also because it would give their
children a proper place to live.   For a time Gill retained a
studio in Chelsea, in order to be closer to the working cli-
mate of a stone-cutter, but this too was outgrown.   Workshops were then set up at Ditchlings in the form of a guild.
Later, the guild was enlarged and named St. Dominic's.

Questions of philosophy, sociology, and religion began
to peck at the doorsill of Gill's mind.   He continued to think
and write and discuss.   The unanimity of thought that had
graced the Lincoln's Inn discussions--habits of questioning
without heat, rationally searching--brought about slow change.
Inexorably a religion was born in Gill's mind to which his
whole being subscribed.   He tells us that he was horrified
to find that this religion was the Roman Catholic religion.
The horrors, however, proved incidental in the face of absolute certainty.   Gill and his family were received into the
Church in 1913 on his twenty-ninth birthday.

In one way Gill's life from this point typifies the
Pauline definition of Baptism: "a rebirth in Christ."   For
Eric Gill, daily living became colored, drawn, and deeply
textured by Catholic principles.   The life of the Church be-
came his life; his life became a vital part of the Church.
By 1922 Gill's total immersion in the living history of Roman

Catholicism led him to found, with three of his friends and
their families, a kind of medieval guild: St. Dominic's at
Ditchlings in Sussex.   Earlier, Gill had become a Third
Order Dominican--binding himself to a way of life set apart.
But now this small group went further, though they were
never bound to Ditchlings by vow.   It was a simple agree-
ment to observe a common life; to include, when possible,
the prayers and rites of the Church as part of daily living;
to set up workshops so that work would be a joy and joy
their work.

     This new move brought an end to the struggle with
art and sculpture.   The popularity of his stone-carving
(actually stone sculptures) had placed Gill among artistic
dilettantes whose aim seemed to be "Art for Art's Sake."
These empty discussions first confused and then distressed
Gill.   Ditchlings made it possible for Gill to be independent
of Art, with a capital A.   Not that Gill, at Ditchlings, no
longer used stone sculpturing as a means, but the end became different; his revolution was in full swing.[3]

     Gill the Workman became a reality with facets so
varied and ends so simple that his life forms a beautiful design.   From here on Gill is simultaneously a wood-engraver,
typographer, designer, sculptor, author, lecturer and some-
time commentator.

     The ideals which prompted the workshops at St.
Dominic's remained untarnished by time but the reality of
living there became a near-hell for the Gill family.   In his
Autobiography Gill tells little of the mechanizations of men
which brought this about.   But we know from him that it
became a show-place disturbed by the avid curiosity of on-
lookers.   And so, in 1924, arose another circumstance,
another change.

Four years in the Black Mountains of Wales healed
the ravages of publicity.   Peace, strength, and purpose were
allowed to grow and mould and enfold in quiet seclusion.
Three families lived on the property of an old deserted abbey.
Each remained autonomous but each contributed to the whole.
Workshops were established and the entire wants of the group
were produced on the farm.   Mary Ethel Gill was largely
responsible for this.

There were two other moves in Gill's life that brought
special influences to his work.   From time to time the cli-
mate and out-of-door work on monuments affected his health;
under doctor's orders he rested and worked periodically in
a sunny village on the coast of France, Salies de Bearn.
The second move was of a more permanent nature.   Capel-
y-ffin in Wales had been chosen deliberately in a flight from
civilization.   It was nearly inaccessible.   The ride from the
railroad to the Abbey was possible only on mule-back.   This
presented a problem for freight, especially heavy stone carv-
ings, etc.   Furthermore, the increased demands being made
for designing and lettering indicated a location nearer to
London.   The Gill families (two sons-in-law and their families and families of two friends) had been renting the Abbey
in Wales.   Increased means (by ordinary standards, not
much) made a down payment possible, so the group moved
to Pigotts.

From the time that Gill had taken his first lettering
job in 1902 he was never without all of the work he was able
to do.   First he became a stone-mason, a carver of monuments and inscriptions;   later a stone-carver, a sculptor who
carved his dreams;   and still later, a letterer, a letter-
designer who placed his letters in patterns on pages in books.

Gill wrote books, some of which other people designed and some for which he created designs himself.   The history of these designs and their singularity interrupts his biography at this point because they were so much a part of his life.

Notes

1.   Eric Gill.   <u>Autobiography</u>.   London: Jonathan Cape, 1940, 286p.   This reference was the first source for the information in this chapter.

2.   Eric Gill.   <u>Letters</u>.   Walter Shewring, ed.   London: Jonathan Cape, 1947, 480p.   This reference added detailed insight into Gill's life which the <u>Autobiography</u> treated in a cursory manner.

3.   All of the Gill writings listed in the Bibliography of this book contributed to this author's understanding of the struggle and expressed beliefs of Eric Gill.   They were not incorporated into the footnotes specifically because these impressions were not particularized.

CHAPTER 3

PRESS DESIGNS, 1927-1940

Gill designs from miscellaneous presses are not all
imposing when considered in the context of fine printing and
limited editions, yet enough of them are to delineate his
stature as a designer. The more specifically "fine presses"
continue the delineation which is completed by designs produced at Pigotts, the Gill workshops.

The first books to be considered are included to complete the survey of work between 1927 and 1940. They are
titles which will be of interest because of their content.
They are: Art and a Changing Civilization (The Bodley Head,
1934); Eric Gill, Autobiography (Jonathan Cape Ltd., 1940);
Beauty Looks After Herself (Sheed and Ward, 1933); Christianity and Art (Shakespeare Head Press, 1928); Christianity
and the Machine Age (Sheldon Press, 1940); The Future of
Sculpture (Lanston Monotype Corporation Press, 1928); The
New Temple Shakespeare (J. M. Dent and Sons, 1934-1936);
and Work and Leisure (Faber and Faber, 1935). [1]

Only The New Temple Shakespeare is, of all of these,
a notable production, and that because of its size--five inches
by four inches. It nestles in the palm of one's hand or in
the corner of one's pocket as if it belongs. The contrast between this seeming preciousness and the large clear type is

18

but a whisper of the artistry for which one is searching.
But it is a whisper.   There are forty volumes, each with
its appropriate engraving personifying tragedy, comedy, history, or romance, done either in the cheap edition in red
cloth at two shillings or in the more expensive binding of
limp black leather for three shillings.

Both the Autobiography and Beauty Looks After Herself
are graced by the use of Gill's Perpetua type   (to be analyzed
as a design-tool in the fifth chapter).   Suffice it to say at
this point that Perpetua is considered one of the most readable of the twentieth-century types.

There are five more books in the miscellaneous press
group to be considered: Art and Love (Douglas Cleverdon,
1927);   Art-Nonsense and Other Essays (Cambridge University Press, 1929);   Clothes (Jonathan Cape, 1931);   Engravings (Fanfare Press, 1929);   and The Song of the Soul (Chis-
wick Press, 1927).

Art and Love was limited to two hundred and sixty
copies, thirty-five of which were sold at two guineas, full-
bound in vellum and autographed by the artist-author.   The
whole edition was printed in eleven point Caslon Old Face
on Batchelor handmade paper which had an oakleaf watermark.
The six full-page illustrations were copper engravings by
Gill, an extra set of which were included in the more expensive edition.   The ordinary copies were bound in black buckram and sold for half the price of the better bindings.   The
press work was done at the Golden Cockerel but for the
Douglas Cleverdon Publishing house.   This was one of the
few instances when Gill used copper instead of wood.

The twenty-four essays of Art-Nonsense were produced in three formats: one impression on large paper

(ten by six inches), a second on ordinary sized paper (nine
by five-and-one-half inches), and the last termed Cassell's
Pocket Library (six and three-fourths by four and one-fourth
inches).   The various sizes had different bindings and prices
but the element that set this book apart was its use of Perpetua Roman and Felicity italic type, both Gill designs.

Three years later the special edition of Clothes, bound
in pigskin and fawn colored boards and selling for one guinea,
and the ordinary edition bound in green cloth with the top
edges dyed green, selling for ten shillings and a sixpence,
created quite a stir.   Perpetua was beginning to be known
and acclaimed.

Fanfare Press worked together with Gill to secure the
blocks and permission from former publishers to produce a
bound volume of his Engravings.   It was not the price (ten
full-bound volumes selling for thirty guineas each; eighty in
bindings of one-fourth vellum and boards, selling at ten
guineas; and four hundred in black cloth bindings for five
guineas) that made this book a collector's item.   It was
above all the material itself and the controversy it provoked.
The controversy begun by the preface and carried on in various journals and papers of the day helped to establish Gill's
place as a spokesman for book design.

The last book to be considered in this group is a
minor achievement, The Song of the Soul.   Its appearance
taken as a whole is that of a small but not too valuable
jewel.   The twenty-four pages measuring eight and one-half
by eleven inches are bound in one-fourth red buckram and
batik boards, and include four full-page wood engravings in
the general format.   The combination of engravings and type
patterns is especially satisfying.

Douglas Pepler, Gill's partner and friend in St. Dominic Press publications, wrote A Letter from Sussex in lieu of a personal appearance at a Gill exhibit in Chicago in 1950. He said that early in 1926 the "Golden Cockerel began to crow on his (Gill's) doorstep, offering expensive editions deliberately enhanced by the skill of eye and hand of a master."[2] The Golden Cockerel Press had been born in Berkshire in 1920 with a two-fold objective: "to print and publish in a cooperative manner and under the conditions of a village industry, new works of literary significance by young authors; and to print and publish fine editions of books of established worth."[3] Mr. Robert Gibbings purchased the press in 1924 from Harold M. Taylor and continued working for the same objectives until 1934 when he retired. At that time Christopher Sandford took over the direction of the press. It soon came to be acknowledged by the critics that the work of the Golden Cockerel, while good, was no longer in the category of fine printing. However, Gill's association with the press was limited to the regime of Robert Gibbings. His collaboration resulted in limited editions which were generally conceded to be lovely.

Still, two of the three books written by Gill and published by Golden Cockerel are just better than average designs. These are Art and Prudence (Golden Cockerel, 1928) and Clothing Without Cloth (Golden Cockerel, 1933). But The Lord's Song, a long slim book in design, is exceptional. Its twenty-four pages of Arnold and Foster's pure rag paper are the setting for exquisitely placed fourteen point Perpetua and Felicity. This book, bound in white buckram, five hundred copies of which sold for two shillings and a sixpence, has an overall harmony and an allusive quality that makes it a delight to see.

Of the other nine Golden Cockerel publications, only
two were unremarkable: The Constant Mistress by Enid Clay
(Golden Cockerel, 1934) and Utopia, a reprint of Robynson's
1556 edition of the Thomas More classic (1929).

The lesser lights among the remaining seven are not
easy to pick because the glow is so constant and so sure
from each of them. The folio of Geoffrey Chaucer's Canterbury Tales is an example of this point. Two hundred and
sixty-seven wood-engraved borders, designed by Gill as a
setting for the eighteen point Caslon Old Face have the im-
pact of living tradition. The vellum edition, full-bound by
Sangorsky and Sutcliff in black morocco (thirty pounds, five
shillings) and the one-fourth bound in red morocco and patterned boards, boxed in red (six guineas), are equally lovely.
The Gill designs blend every word and every page (printed
on handmade Batchelor paper with the Cockerel watermark).
This is a work of exquisite harmony (see plate II).

The Four Gospels (Golden Cockerel, 1931) is another
such design although it is more awkwardly executed in eighteen point Golden Cockerel type especially designed by Gill
for the press. The book is a folio (thirteen and one-half by
nine inches) of great bulk with sixty-four wood-engraved illustrations interwoven throughout the text. A detailed analysis of this and of the design of Glue and Lacquer by Harold
Acton and Lee Yi-Hsieh (Golden Cockerel, 1941) is reserved
for other chapters (see plate VI).

The Green Ship (Golden Cockerel, 1936) also presents
outstanding design. Uniquely, it makes use of the double-
page title spread using wood engravings of six characters
caught in the sweep of mighty waves. Thirteen point Perpetua
type is printed on British mould-made paper or vellum in

For every clerk anon right heeld with other.
They seyde, 'the man is wood, my leve brother';
And every wight gan laughen of this stryf.
Thus swyved was the carpenteres wyf,
For al his keping and his Ialousye;
And Absolon hath kist hir nether ye;
And Nicholas is scalded in the toute.
This tale is doon, and God save al the route!

WHAN folk had laughen at this nyce cas
Of Absolon and hende Nicholas,
Diverse folk diversely they seyde;
But, for the more part, they loughe and pleyde,
Ne at this tale I saugh no man him greve,
But it were only Osewold the Reve,

132

PLATE II. Eric Gill. The Reeves Tale. The Canterbury
Tales, 4 vols. Golden Cockerel Press, 1928. p. 132 of
vol. 1.

three bindings: full-bound green boards (two guineas), or
full-bound morocco on vellum (fifty guineas). Zacknsdorf
did the four vellum copies while Sangorsky and Sutcliff did
the remaining editions.

Troilus and Creseyde (Golden Cockerel, 1927), another
Chaucer, preceded The Canterbury Tales in time as a publication and was less important as book design. However,
it was the first clarion call announcing design possibilities
in Gill work. The three hundred and twenty pages in eighteen point Caslon Old Face were traditionally set in sixty
wood-engraved borders printed on Kelmscott handmade paper
watermarked with a hammer and anvil. The borders and the
five full-page illustrations were printed with twenty initials
and four tail pieces in three colors, red, blue and black.
Theodore Besterman's Travels and Sufferings of Brebeuf
(Golden Cockerel, 1938) was remarkable because of its title
page and type: the first a double-page spread using two
colors and six blocks for the wood engraving, and the latter
the new sixteen point Bembo monotype designed by Gill.

Late in 1928 Gill and René Hague began the foundation
of a press of their own at North Dean, High Wycombe. The
press was actually only a part of a cooperative enterprise
projected by three Catholic craftsmen and their families as
a series of workshops and domiciles, not unlike the plan of
the medieval guilds. The participants were united by a common goal, a common enterprise, and a common rule of life.
In a letter to his friend Rev. Desmond Chute, Gill described
the original setup before remodeling began: "... a clearing
in a 'forest' of about eighteen acres in the midst whereof is
a courtyard of buildings with red-tiled roofs: this is Pigotts
and consists of a courtyard surrounded by erstwhile farm

buildings--viz: two large barns, stables, etc. , and a farm
house and two cottages. "[4]

A statement of The Eric Gill Workshops published on
December 5, 1940 explained: "It was the lifelong desire of
Eric Gill to be given the power to found something which
would go on working after his death. (He died in November.)
His aim was that Pigotts should become the enduring home of
craftsmanship. For this purpose he trained his journeymen
and tried to establish the physical and spiritual conditions
which make good work possible...."[5]   Gill did good work
himself under these conditions and for this reason the books
printed at Pigotts from 1931 until his death are a kind of
climax to this survey. In fact, the Hague and Gill press
work forms the backbone of the mature design work of Gill.

Pigotts made use of a handpress, hand-set type, handmade paper especially watermarked and type especially designed by Gill for his press. René Hague was his partner
and his pressman as well as his son-in-law. Denis Terget-
meir, also a son-in-law, was a journeyman and illustrator,
and Gordian Gill, his son and apprentice, completed the ros-
trum of associates who signed the aforementioned statement.

In another letter, this time to the Monotype Recorder
in 1933, Gill refutes the idea that Pigotts was a "private
press": "It would be strictly correct to say that we have
started a printing business: the style of the firm being
'Hague and Gill, Printers'.... The real distinction between
such a press and others is not in the typographical quality
of the work it does nor in the typographical enthusiasms of
the proprietors, but simply in the fact that a 'private press'
prints solely what it chooses to print, whereas a public press
prints what its customers demand of it. "[6] Pigotts was a

upon a rock. And every one that heareth these sayings of mine, and doeth them not, shall be likened unto a foolish man, which built his house upon the sand: And the rain descended, and the floods came, and the winds blew, and beat upon that house; and it fell: and great was the fall of it.

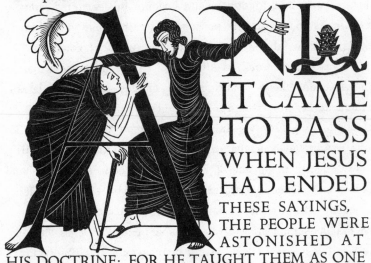

AND IT CAME TO PASS WHEN JESUS HAD ENDED THESE SAYINGS, THE PEOPLE WERE ASTONISHED AT HIS DOCTRINE: FOR HE TAUGHT THEM AS ONE HAVING AUTHORITY, AND NOT AS THE SCRIBES. WHEN he was come down from the mountain, great multitudes followed him. And, behold, there came a leper and worshipped him, saying, Lord, if thou wilt, thou canst make me clean. And Jesus put forth his hand, and touched him, saying, I will; be thou clean. And immediately his leprosy was cleansed. And Jesus saith unto him, See thou tell no man; but go thy way, shew thyself to the priest, and offer the gift that Moses commanded, for a testimony unto them. ✳ And when Jesus was entered into

PLATE III.　Eric Gill.　The Leper.　The Four Gospels. Golden Cockerel Press, 1931.　p. 20.

business, but it was a business bound up in a way of life.
In this atmosphere of liturgical living the group worked
freely, joyously, and with amazing success.

The first book under consideration, The Lost Child
by Mulk Raj Anand (J. A. Allen and Company, 1934), and
the next three--Sculpture and the Living Model (Sheed and
Ward, 1932), Trousers (Faber and Faber, Ltd. , 1937) and
The Unholy Trinity (J. M. Dent and Sons, 1938), all by
Gill--were paperbacks. Both the first book and Trousers
were printed in twelve point Joanna type. The last named
book had no title page but the title statement and imprint
were placed inside of the front wrapper. Each book in this
group sold for one shilling.

Sculpture and the Living Model was printed in eight
point Gill Extra Light Sans-Serif, which seems to belie the
idea expressed by Gill that the sans-serif types were not
suitable book types. The Unholy Trinity was unique in type
also. Fourteen point Bunyan (a Gill design) helped to cate-
gorize this little book as no slight achievement.

Three more works written by Gill must be mentioned
in connection with his designs; however, they do not repre-
sent important book designs. They are Drawings from Life
(Kimble and Bradford, 1940), Engravings (Faber and Faber,
1934) and Twenty-five Nudes (J. M. Dent and Sons, 1939).
These collections are visual catalogs of Gill's art work.

Aldous Huxley, on the second page of his introduction
to Printing Today, says: "by someone who understands his
business the printed page can be composed into patterns almost as satisfyingly beautiful as those of a carpet or a bro-
cade. "[7]

The Workshops of Hague and Gill evolved a

characteristic title page which became a symbol of Gill's work. The three titles following, which were books written by Gill as well as designed by him, are examples: <u>Money and Morals</u> (Faber and Faber, Ltd. , 1934), <u>Sacred and Secular</u> (J. M. Dent and Sons, 1937), and <u>Work and Property</u> (J. M. Dent and Sons, 1937). The pattern of the page combined the Title Page with the Table of Contents in a simple and beautiful form (see plate IV). Each of these books, printed in twelve point Joanna, bound in colored cloth and sold for six shillings, exemplifies the Gill contention that the binding was the least important point to be considered in book design; and where expense had to be limited, fine binding was sacrificed but not fine type, fine paper, or fine design.

The remaining eight books designed by Gill must be considered individually because each design is an achievement in itself.

Gill believed that justification of the right hand margin was less important than retaining the even flow of letters, and one finds an excellent example of this theory practically applied in <u>An Essay on Typography</u> (Sheed and Ward, 1931), a book on type and its problems, written by Gill. The appearance of this book in twelve point Joanna, printed on handmade paper especially watermarked ER, with the E reversed, and bound in red buckram on green cloth, was not as imposing as its reception by the press might indicate. Even the jacket was declared a departure in design. There was a limited edition of twenty-five copies bound by Donald Atwater in Welsh sheepskin, blind-tooled front and back with the Hague and Gill press mark (see plates V and VI). In this edition one sees that where expense permits, the whole

SACRED & SECULAR &c / by ERIC GILL

containing

and eight illustrations by Denis Tegetmeier

LONDON / J. M. DENT & SONS LTD

FOR HAGUE & GILL LTD / 1940

PLATE IV. Hague and Gill. Title page. <u>Sacred and Secular</u>. J. M. Dent and Sons, Ltd. , 1940.

book design is an allusive triumph.

The colophon of the next selection to be considered tells its story succinctly: "This edition of Hamlet is designed and illustrated by Eric Gill. Fifteen hundred copies have been printed from the Joanna type on Barcham Green paper by Hague and Gill, High Wycombe, for the members of the Limited Editions Club, 1933." But this does not express the exquisite poetry of the book's format: strong deep-textured leather binding of golden tan pigskin, blind stamped with the dog and tree press marks; exquisitely dainty type, patterned allusively to express mounting tension, emotion, and tragedy; the wood engravings set into the page designs like minor climaxes in the drama. All in all, this book is a joy to handle, a pleasure to see.

The high point in Gill design was reached in the production of the Aldine Bible. The unusual format of this edition of the New Testament (J. M. Dent and Sons, Ltd., 1934-1935, four volumes), measuring seven and three-fourths inches by four and seven-eighths inches, personifies function and simplicity. The volumes bound in limp red leather sold for seven shillings and sixpence, while those bound in dark red Sundour cloth sold for five shillings. The use of twelve point Joanna type on this size of Barcham Green handmade paper seems to be perfect in porportion. Verse divisions are disregarded except for reference headings at the top of the page. Speeches are indicated by a comma followed by a capital letter; quotations from the Old Testament are included in single quotes; the notes are all grouped at the back of the volume concerned, and are printed in Joanna italic. Each element in these books works alone and with every other element within the whole design to produce a

(cont'd on p. 34)

Printed by

Rene Hague & Eric Gill

PLATE V. Hague and Gill. Printer's Mark--Book Jacket.
An Essay on Typography. Sheed and Ward, 1931, exterior.

¶ As to what does or should sell, we may say that the things which should form the shape & proportions of the page are the hand and the eye: the hand because books of wide proportions are unwieldy to hold: and the eye because lines of more than 10-12 words are awkward to read. (With longer lines, set solid, i.e. without leads between them, there is difficulty in following from one line to the next, &, even if the type be leaded, a long line necessitates a distinctly felt muscular movement of the eye and, in extreme cases, of the head.) As to the height of a page, this again is governed by the needs of hand & eye: a very tall page necessitates either a distinct movement of the neck of the reader or a changing of the angle at which the book is held in the hand, & such things are simply a nuisance. It may be that there are other considerations than those of physical convenience which have helped to determine the normal octavo page: it may be that such a proportion is intrinsically pleasing to the human mind. It is, however, sufficient for us to see that there is a physical reasonableness in this proportion, and we may safely leave the discovery of other reasons to professional aestheticians.

¶ The shape of the page being given, it remains to

discover the best proportions for the lines & mass of type printed upon it. Here again physical considerations are a sufficient guide. Two things are to be thought of: the type & the margins. Let us consider the margins first. The inner margin exists simply to separate a page from the one opposite to it, and need be no wider than is enough to keep the printed words clear of the bend of the paper where it is sewn in binding. The top margin, again, needs only to be sufficiently wide to isolate the type from the surrounding landscape of furniture and carpets (just as a 'mount' or frame is used by painters to isolate a picture from wall paper, &c.). On the other hand, the outer and bottom margins need more width than is required for mere isolation, for it is by these margins that the book is held in the hand: enough must be allowed for thumbs, and the bottom margins need more than the side or outer ones. These physical considerations being allowed for, we may now consider the margins in relation to one another, & it will be seen at once that, taking one page at a time, i.e. half the 'opening', slightly more must be allowed to the top margin than is required for mere isolation: for if you make the top and inner margins equally narrow, the outer mar-

PLATE VI.   Eric Gill.   Typography.   An Essay on Typography.   Sheed and Ward, 1931.   p. 108-109.

PLATE VII. Eric Gill. <u>Hamlet</u>--colophon. Limited Editions Club, 1933, end page.

readable New Testament, and each element alone and as a
part of the whole spells beauty.

In spite of poor binding The Holy Sonnets by John
Donne (J. M. Dent and Sons Ltd. , 1938) achieved no slight
notice.   The beautiful clear character of Bunyan type (a Gill
design) is in perfect harmony with the mind of the poet ex-
pressing clear and beautiful images;   strange but lovely wood
engravings drift through the text design like disembodied
spirits;   page after page is patterned in balanced simplicity.
These points of the book's design won acclaim almost immediately.

The Passion of Our Lord taken from the four evange-
lists (Faber and Faber, Ltd. , 1934), with Latin and English
texts on alternating pages, measuring seven inches by four,
is important because of its use of eight point Joanna type.
In this small form the letters are both clear and exquisite.
Although the printing is done on Barcham Green handmade
paper, following Gill's policy of unjustified right hand margins, with five full-page wood engravings, the book is not a
completely successful pocket edition.   The type is too small
for much of it to be read with ease.

The Passion of Perpetua and Felicity (Douglas Cleverdon, 1932) was not printed first as a book;   Hague and Gill
did it as an insert for The Fleuron magazine.   Its publication (exactly the same in every detail) as a book bound in
one-fourth vellum and black paper boards was limited to
thirty copies at one pound, eleven shillings and sixpence.
Today this book is a collector's item, not because of the
binding (always a negligible item in Gill's eyes) but because
a new book-type created by him for the Lanston Monotype
Corporation was used for the first time in The Passion of
(cont'd on p. 38)

THE PASSION OF
PERPETUA AND
FELICITY

MARTYRED AT CARTHAGE A.D. CCIII

A NEW TRANSLATION BY

W. H. SHEWRING

WITH ENGRAVINGS ON WOOD

BY

ERIC GILL

London, 1929

PRINTED FOR 'THE FLEURON'

in Perpetua roman made by the

Lanston Monotype Corporation from the design of

ERIC GILL

¶ This book is designed by Eric Gill, the pages being composed in a new type created by him expressly for this book. The illustrations are etchings by Denis Tegetmeier. The printing is done by Hague & Gill, High Wycombe, England; and fifteen hundred copies have been made for the members of The Limited Editions Club,

this copy being number

1319.

and signed by

ERIC G and *Denis T*

PLATE IX.   Eric Gill.   <u>A Sentimental Journey</u>--Colophon.
The Limited Editions Club, 1936, end page.

S O oft have I invok'd thee for my Muse,

And found such faire assistance in my verse,

As every Alien pen hath got my use,

And under thee their poesie disperse.

Thine eyes, that taught the dumbe on high to sing,

And heavie ignorance aloft to flie,

Have added fethers to the learneds wing,

And given grace a double Majestie.

Yet be most proud of that which I compile,

Whose influence is thine, and borne of thee,

In others workes thou doost but mend the stile,

And Arts with thy sweete graces graced be.

But thou art all my art, and doost advance

As high as learning, my rude ignorance.

PLATE X.   The Sonnets of William Shakespeare.   Cassell
and Company, Ltd. , 1933.   p. 78

Perpetua and Felicity. Perpetua Roman and Felicity italic
were recognized by Stanley Morison as contemporary types
of distinction and promise[8] (see Plate VIII).

The Colophon of A Sentimental Journey by Laurence
Sterne (Limited Editions Club, 1936) states, "this book is
designed by Eric Gill, the pages being composed in new
type created by him expressly for this book" (see Plate IX).
Actually the publication of this book preceded The Holy
Sonnets (also in Bunyan type) by two years. It became
another strong rung in the ladder of achievement for Gill.

A pocket-sized edition of The Sonnets of William
Shakespeare (Cassel and Company, 1933) was printed in
twelve point Joanna on Basingwerk paper and sold for ten
shillings.   Though five hundred copies of this work were
published early in the history of the Gill Workshops, as a
design it is last and not least in this survey. This is because Gill realized, in Joanna italic, his aim "to produce
not an accompaniment for, nor a contrast to, Joanna Roman
but a true italic type, i. e. , one whose slight slope is necessitated by desire to make a narrow but not a condensed letter. "[9] Alone, and with wide leading, the new design is
clear and interesting, but its use as an italic for combination
with Roman will be considered in the next chapter.

Notes

1.   Each book cited in this survey has been actually handled and
       minutely examined with this in mind. The Gill collec-
       tion at the Clark Memorial Library of the Univ. of Cal.
       at Los Angeles provided the opportunity: The Bibliog-
       raphy of Eric Gill by Evan Gill (Cassell and Company
       Ltd. , 1953) provided the verifications.

2.   H. D. C. Pepler.   A Letter From Sussex.   Chicago:

Society of Typographic Arts, 1950.   p. 3.

3.   G. S. Tomkinson.   A Select Bibliography of Modern
       Presses.   London: The First Editions Club, 1928.

4.   Eric Gill.   Letters.   Walter Shewring, ed.   New York:
       Devin-Adair, 1948.   p. 236.

5.   Gordian Gill.   The Eric Gill Workshops.   Pigotts:
       Hague and Gill, 1940.   p. 2.

6.   Eric Gill.   Op. cit. , p. 282.

7.   Aldous Huxley.   "Introduction," Printing Today by Simon
       Oliver.   London: Peter Davies, Ltd.   p. 2.

8.   Stanley Morison.   The Fleuron VII: 29-44, 1929.

9.   Special note following page 155 of The Sonnets of William
       Shakespeare.   Margaret Flower, editor.

CHAPTER 4

TRADITIONAL FORCES
IN GILL BOOK DESIGNS

The general survey of Gill's book designs in chapter
three did not delineate the historical backgrounds of his work,
nor did it underline those characteristics of his design that
derived from tradition in typography.   This chapter aims to
accomplish both of these objectives, as well as to present
the place of five traditional forms used as a basis of creative endeavor by Eric Gill.   These five forms are: 1) Roman capitals as found on the Trajan column;   2) Insular
minuscules, a source of lower-case letters as seen on a
page from The Book of Kells; 3) The earliest Roman types
exemplified by pages from books designed by Jenson and by
Sweynheim and Pannartz;   4) the Aldine tradition of Roman,
italic and Greek letters;   5) the newer forms of Roman type
created by Baskerville and Caslon.

The place of tradition as a force in typographic history is subject to the perennial controversy of "period piece
versus modern" in the art world of each successive genera-
tion.   The definitions of traditional and contemporary design
make it clear that the exact imitation of the type form of
any particular era, taken out of the context of its age, makes
for static work.

To be specific, in 1909 Gill prepared five plates to

be included in Edward Johnson's portfolio <u>Manuscript and
Inscription Letters for Schools and Classes and for the Use
of Craftsmen.</u> [1] How nearly he captured at this time the
spirit and the form of early Roman capitals may be seen by
comparing plate XI, a facsimile of an actual photograph of
part of the Trajan column, with plates XII and XIII which are
facsimiles of Gill's free drawing made from a similar photograph found in the Victoria and Albert Museum.   There is
for the most part great likeness in form: note the narrow
"E," the widespread "M," the thin "C," and the sturdy "G."
Gill tilts his "O" slightly and shortens his "L." Feel the
restraint, the noble lines and the proportionate relationships
of strokes and letters formed by sharp tools on hard stone
(a reality in both cases because Gill was a stone-cutter long
before he thought of designing book letters).

　　　Later in this book it may become apparent that from
this incisive spirit of Roman lettering Gill built new forms,
but these particular plates only hold a promise of future de-
velopment in type.   It shows quite clearly "Roman capitals
... suitable for ordinary sign writing."[2]

　　　<u>The Book of Kells</u>, a manuscript controversially at-
tributed from the sixth to the ninth centuries, personifies the
insular minuscule as the beginning and first-flowering of our
lower-case alphabet[3] (see plate XIV, a facsimile reproduction
of a page from the Verlag edition of <u>The Book of Kells</u>).
(Compare plate XII and plate XIII with the minuscule.) Nothing that Gill did approaches the radiant harmony of these
forms, although throughout Gill's work as a designer of books
one finds this same clarity of spirit.   Only a few of the
forms, "d," "p," "c," "u," and "e" are easily recognizable.
Golden Cockerel Type (plate III) and Perpetua (plate VIII)

achieve a degree of this radiant effect, though neither these
nor Bunyan (plate XVIII) have the same close alliance between
letters as have those of the Irish monks at Kells.   Most certainly they are not in any sense of the word direct imitators
of the traditional minuscule letter forms.

The forces of tradition have been defined here as
"living powers in the present which transmit the past. "[4]
Literally, tradition means the act of handing down re-vitalized
forms, type forms in this instance.   Roman letters of the
Trajan Inscription of lowercase letters of the Carolingian
minuscule became traditional forces in later centuries only
when they were used in relation to new problems in new
ages; ages which adapted them to their needs and spirit,
transforming them and strengthening them. [5]

Jensen did this, as did Sweynheim and Pannartz,
though neither stone inscription nor manuscript lettering as
such concerned them.   Their problem was a result of their
own age: an adaptation of humanistic letters to type.   At
that time designers were using manuscripts as evaluative
criteria when judging type, but were these forms particularly,
creatively new, transformed or strengthened?   It appears to
be so.   The revival of interest in classical learning led to
a kind of distillation: a distillation drawn from comparisons
of ninth-century Carolingian manuscripts and fifteenth-century manuscripts which became in the work of Jenson and
of Sweynheim and Pannartz, the basis of a new tradition,
Roman type.

Analyzing their Roman type letter by letter, one finds
each form far from perfect in a mechanical sense but the
evenness of the mass and the interrelationships established
between letters result in a page design that is hard to equal
(cont'd on p. 48)

PLATE XI. Facsimile of photograph. The Trajan Column,
114 A.D. James Hayes. Roman Letter. (R. R. Donnelly).
1951-52, p. 15.

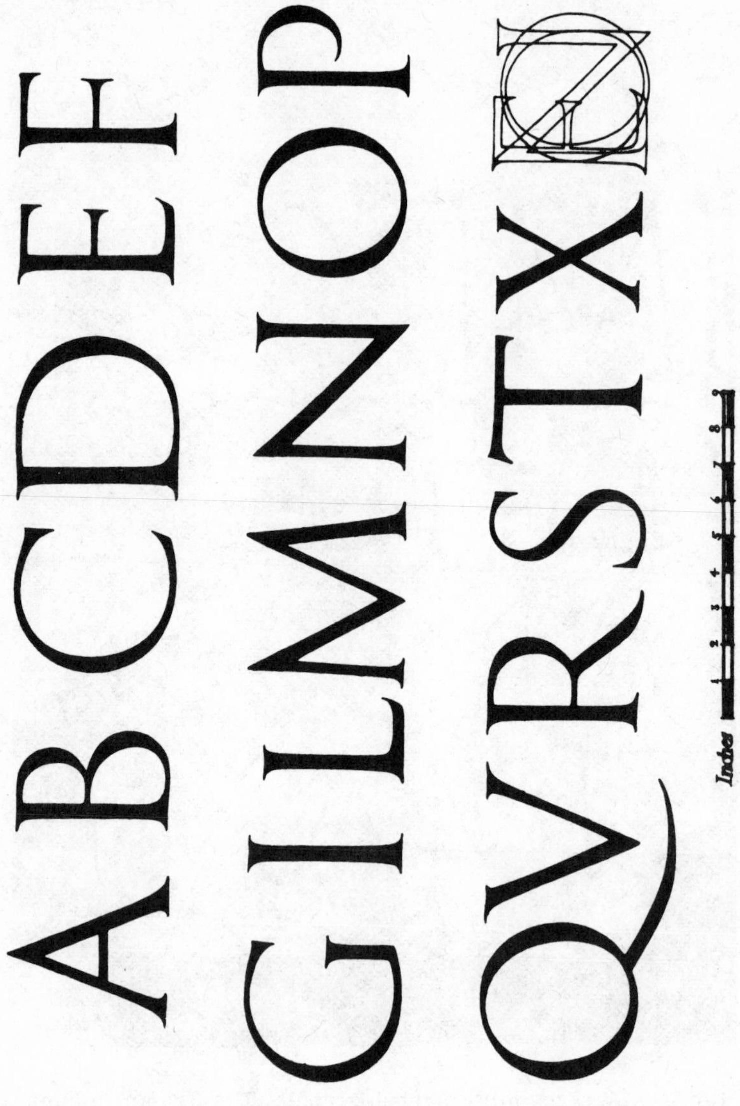

PLATE XII.   Eric Gill.   The Trajan Column.   Manuscript
and Inscription Letters for Schools and Classes and Craftsmen (John Hogg), 1909, plate 12 (one of five done for
Edward Johnson).

PLATE XIII. Eric Gill. Based on the Trajan Column. Manuscript and Inscription Letters (John Hogg), 1909, plate 13 (one of five done for Edward Johnson).

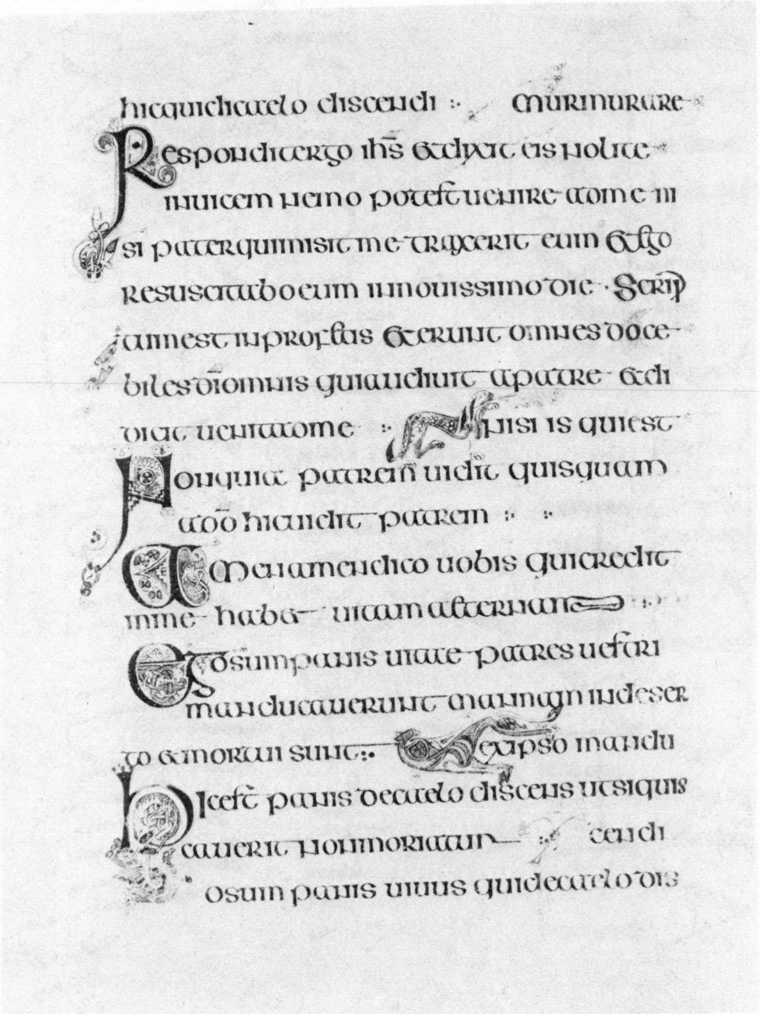

hic qui de caelo discendi :: murmurare
Respondit ergo ihs et dixit eis nolite
inuicem nemo potest uenire ad me ni
si pater qui missit me traxerit eum et ego
resuscitabo eum in nouissimo die · Scrip
tum est in profetis et erunt omnes doce
biles di omnis qui audiuit a patre et di
dicit uenit ad me :: Nisi is qui est
Non quia patrem uidit quisquam
a dō hic uidit patrem :: ::
Amen amen dico uobis qui credit
in me habet uitam aeternam ::
Ego sum panis uitae patres uestri
manducauerunt manna in deser
to et mortui sunt :: ex ipso mandu
Hic est panis de caelo discens ut si quis
cauerit non moriatur :: cendi
Ego sum panis uiuus qui de caelo dis

PLATE XIV. Photocopy of facsimile. John: VI, 42-53. The Book of Kells (ninth-century Irish manuscript). Bern: Urs Graf-Verlag.

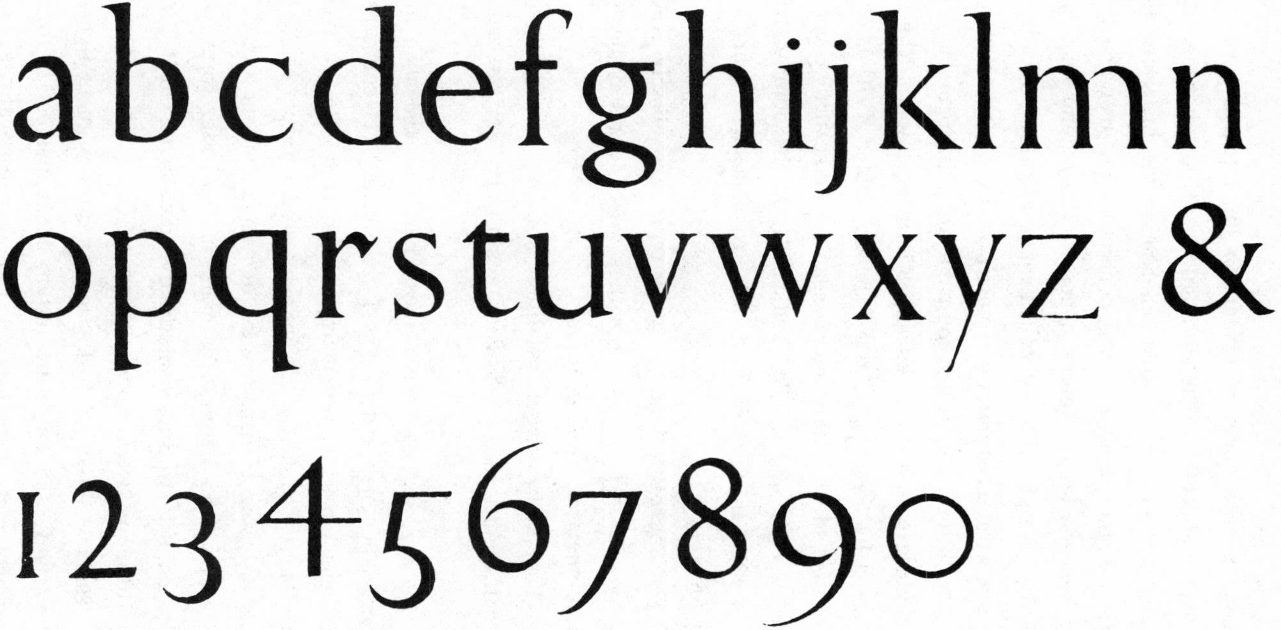

abcdefghijklmn
opqrstuvwxyz &
1234567890

PLATE XV. Eric Gill. Letters drawn for Perpetua type design.

because of a consequent movement of the integral parts (see plates XVI and XVII). The distinctions evident between the two plates are characteristics inherent in the creations them- selves. Jenson's type is more controlled in form and the affinity between forms seems deeper. Sweynheim and Pan- nartz' page design is laced with broad capitals, with sturdy serifs and with irregularities, yet it retains a classical grace. Letter for letter, the pages compare alike in form but with that individualism that marks an artistic creation. The al- phabet used by Sweynheim and Pannartz (plate XVII) is seen to be composed of letters more nearly square than round ex- cept in the case of "o," "q" and "p." On the other hand, Jenson's work is marked by a semi-roundness, a more con- densed form.

The sources, then, of these types are clearly tradi- tional, but within their own age they were definitely modern and quite certainly new in form.

The last two pages establish two forces in printing to have been traditional. How does a similar Gill type measure up?

Bunyan, a type design created by Gill and used in A Sentimental Journey and in The Holy Sonnets, is comparable to both Jenson's and Sweynheim and Pannartz' Roman type. Placing the traditional pages side by side with plates XVIII and XIX or using transparencies one on top of the other, or inter-linearly, the likeness of many of the letter forms be- comes apparent, while the distinctive quality of Gill's type designs becomes even more obvious.

The full effect of Gill's letters on a page is lighter, more graceful, and letter by letter, more perfect in form. They are not entirely without that interrelationship that one

sees in both the Jenson and in the Sweynheim and Pannartz
plates.   While the consequent movement of parts which depends upon a variation is slighter in the Gill book type, one
also sees a delicate rhythm running through the whole which
acts as a cohesive force for all of the parts (see plate XX).

Furthermore, there is a quality of spirit discernible
in the traditional forms (plates XVI and XVII) that is direct
evidence of their era.   Likewise, there is perceptible to the
eye a deliberate consciousness of the manuscript letter form
and a disregard for the value of type forms as such.   Quite
apparently, the plates exemplifying Gill's design show no evidence of this spirit of the fifteenth century.

One may most certainly conclude from this that while
the Roman type forms of Jenson and of Sweynheim and Pannartz were definite forces influencing the formation of Bunyan
type, it was not a "period piece. "   It does not reflect these
fifteenth-century incunabula done in Roman type nor does it
approximate closely the form of these two traditional types.

To consider yet another possible force in tradition,
the pure contours and the monumental character of Roman
letters as produced by Aldus Manutius in the late fifteenth
and early sixteenth century give him a special place as a
"hander-on" of forms that have a new brilliance, a vibrant
organic life.   Haebler believes that most of the Aldine fonts
were made in imitation of humanistic script but with one
difference: the square Roman capitals were being restudied
and used as the constant companions of the Carolingian minuscule in a manner completely contemporary in quality. [6]
The plate reproduced here (plate XXI) is an example of a
compact face which retains the dignity of Rome while adding
the controlled grace of Venice.   The sturdy straight-backed
(cont'd on p. 56)

ſtus percipies. Sed ſcrob
laxius radices uagentur::
is per anguſtum os penet
eſta eſt:pluuiis non ablu
erint ſpatium habeant:q
ec īfra ſerere qd poteris:ı
inter ordinem quadragɛ
ɔnuenit. Semina lege craſ
a procera ſine ulceribus iı
nt. Si ex ueteribus ramiſ
ıctus afferunt:ac illos mɑ
ıtis conentur. Sed anteq̄
antea erunt conſtitutæ:ʃ

p̃ in urbe nuper aĩrep

Auxit eam:iram poſtı

ertit:audita uox eıuſ:

gẽ Agrariā ferẽtı:ſim

ı.eſſe:q̃ armiſ cepiſſent

:niſi q̃euerint· q̃ audı

cer:nec infacũduſ:nac

ıãq̃ irritãdo agitãdoq̃

q; uniuerſo ordini eſſe

ıũ in diſceptationẽ tra

ıditiſinqt Quiriteſ Sı

uobiſ tãto honore uid

neſturı uestre proſpici

and oft and many a time have I called up by it the courteous spirit of its owner to regulate my own, in the justlings of the world; they had found full employment for his, as I learnt from his story, till about the forty-fifth year of his age, when upon some military services ill requited, and meeting at the same time with a disappointment in the tenderest of passions, he abandoned the sword and the sex together, and took sanctuary, not so much in his convent as in himself.

I feel a damp upon my spirits, as I am going to add, that in my last return through Calais, upon inquiring after Father Lorenzo, I heard he had been dead near three months, and was buried, not in his convent, but, according to his desire, in a little cemetery belonging to it, about two leagues off: I had a strong desire to see where they had laid him—when upon pulling out his little horn box, as I sat by his grave, and plucking up a nettle or two at the head of it, which had no business to grow there, they all struck together so forcibly upon my affections, that I burst into a flood of tears—but I am as weak as a woman; and I beg the world not to smile, but pity me.

The Remise Door——Calais

I HAD never quitted the lady's hand all this time; and had held it so long, that it would have been indecent to have let it go, without first pressing it to my lips: the blood and spirits, which had suffered a revulsion from her, crowded back to her, as I did it.

Now the two travellers, who had spoke to me in the coach-yard, happened at that crisis to be passing by, and observing our communications, naturally took it into their heads that we must be man and wife, at least; so stopping as soon as they came up to the door of the Remise, the one of them, who

PLATE XVIII.   Eric Gill.   <u>A Sentimental Journey</u>.   Limited Editions Club, 1936, p. 21.

X DEATH BE NOT PROUD

XIV

BATTER my heart, three person'd God; for, you
As yet but knocke, breathe, shine, and seeke to mend;
That I may rise, and stand, o'erthrow mee,'and bend
Your force, to breake, blowe, burn and make me new.
I, like an usurpt towne, to'another due,
Labour to'admit you, but Oh, to no end,
Reason your viceroy in mee, mee should defend,
But is captiv'd, and proves weake or untrue.
Yet dearely'I love you,'and would be loved faine,
But am betroth'd unto your enemie:
Divorce mee,'untie, or breake that knot againe,
Take mee to you, imprison mee, for I
Except you'enthrall mee, never shall be free,
Nor ever chast, except you ravish mee.

PLATE XIX.   Eric Gill.   Death Be Not Proud.   The Holy
Sonnets.   J. M. Dent and Sons, 1938, Sonnet XIV.

Nicolas Jenson:
Scriptores Rei
Rusticae - Haebler

Eric Gill:
A Sentimental Journey

Plate XX

Inter-linear Study

Eric Gill:
The Holy Sonnets

Sweynheim and Pannartz
Lividicus Dedicus
Haebler

Eric Gill:
A Sentimental Journey

Eric Gill:
The Holy Sonnets

erint ſpatium habeant:q
ec īfra ſerere qd poteris:r
inter ordinem quadrag

employment for his, as I learnt from his story, till about the forty-fifth year
of his age, when upon some military services ill requited, and meeting at the
same time with a disappointment in the tenderest of passions, he abandoned
the sword and the sex together, and took sanctuary, not so much in his

That I may rise, and stand, o'erthrow mee,'and bend

Your force, to breake, blowe, burn and make me new.

I, like an usurpt towne, to'another due,

cer : nec infacúduſ:nac
iáꝙ irritádo agitádoq
q; uniuerſo ordini eſſe

I feel a damp upon my spirits, as I am going to add, that in my last return
through Calais, upon inquiring after Father Lorenzo, I heard he had been
dead near three months, and was buried, not in his convent, but, according

But is captiv'd, and proves weake or untrue.

Yet dearely'I love you,'and would be loved faine,

But am betroth'd unto your enemie:

stems and the narrower body of the type heightens this illusion of graceful strength.

Two other contributions of Aldus Manutius place his work in the book world on a high plane, namely his italic forms and his Greek fonts.   The italics (the first type in the cursive vernacular) were unique.   They were often copied in later centuries but never with results that were as satisfying.   Indeed, it is the consensus among typographic experts that until the twentieth century no completely satisfactory italic had been created.   The even greater achievement of this printer-designer-publisher lay in his Greek fonts (plate XXII) which were based on the Greek cursive of the day. These too have been unparalleled until recently.   This last plate shows an apparent consonance, a proportionate relationship between letters and a soft clarity that sustains the conviction that Aldus Manutius created traditional types of great beauty.

Furthermore, the book form most often used by Manutius produced a sixteenth-century fad for "pocketbooks." Until this time no one had ever worked to publish a book that was easily handled both physically and financially.   Each of the foregoing factors explains why Manutius became a tradition and remained a tradition.   His place is undisputed in type history, and this because of the vital form which his letters took, even though they were not types distinctly fitted to printing.   But Gill made use of the Aldine tradition, and the following pages will show in just what respects Gill is indebted to Aldus Manutius.

When Gill planned the details of his workshops, he created the design for a basic type for his hand press.   It was to be a Roman type with its own italic form, distinguished

by easy readability and great accessibility.   All of the books,
with but two exceptions, which were printed at Pigotts in the
ten years preceding Gill's death were set in this type. [7]

The three plates selected for study in this connection
are pages from Hamlet (designed and printed for the Limited
Editions Club, 1933), The Aldine Bible (J. M. Dent and Sons
Ltd. , 1934-1936, four volumes) and The Sonnets of William
Shakespeare (Cassell and Company Ltd. , 1933) (see plates
XXIII, XXIV and XXV).

In the photocopy reproductions the "a" and "e" of
Joanna type are inclined to domineer.   This is not true in
the original hand-set pages of these works.   Actually, the
degree of variance between letters is proportionately related
and the white and black forms locked together by sustained
tension are well-balanced.   The over-all effect of a book designed with this type is daintier and, one might also say,
more feminine than one designed with any other book type of
Gill's.   This effect is the result of the weight of the entire
face in direct contrast with the delicate hair lines used in
the serifs.   Fineness does not yield to weakness because of
the quiet dignity of both cases, and only in the italic is there
any barrier to easy readability.

This seems to be true in The Sonnets because of poor
leading.   The note following page 155 of The Sonnets states
Gill's intention "to produce not an accompaniment nor a contrast to the Joanna Roman type but a true italic (i. e. one
whose slight slope is necessitated by the desire to make a
narrow but not a condensed letter). "[8]   Condensation is not
apparent here, but the unfamiliar form of a tall narrow italic
is.   Joanna italic was thus deliberately designed without the
slant which since Aldus has been the primary mark of italic
(cont'd on p. 63)

quando uſcirete del mare tempeſtoſo di queſta tenebroſa uita,& andare
te al loco de ripoſo : & ala uera cita di Hieruſalem.i.uiſion di pace: doue
ogni bene e remunerato:cio e ogni patiétia et bona operatione: la quale
noi adoperiamo in queſta uita. O quáto ſeria matto & ſtolto quello mer
cadante a cui fuſſe meſſo in mano el theſoro per che guadagnaſſe con eſ
ſo:& ello p timore dela pena el ſoteraſſe ſotto la terra.ſerrebbe p certo de
gno di grande reprehenſione & che li fuſſe tolta la uita. Noi ſiamo quel
li mercadanti a cui e commeſſo el theſoro del tempo con lo libero arbi
trio & con la uolunta libera:la quale dio ci ha data & commeſſa per che
noi guadagnamo: pero che mentre che habbiamo el tempo ſiamo acti a
perdere & a guadagnare ſecondo che piace ala uolunta noſtra. Saremo
dunque ſtolti ſe per timore dela pena:& per paura noi ſoteraremo queſto
tempo & queſta uolunta,el quale ci e dato per che noi guadagnamo uita
eterna uiuendo uirtuoſamente,& non ne comperaſſemo l inferno uiué
do uitioſamente:pero che allhora uiue uitioſamente quando ſotera el té
po & la uolunta nela terra:cio e nelo affecto & deſiderio terreno & diſor
dinato fora de dio.Et pero ui dixi chio deſiderauo chel core & lo affecto
uoſtro fuſſe ſpogliato dogni amore & affecto del mondo & timore ſerui
le:& uoglio che ſiati ueſtita ſolo de Chriſto crocifixo:& in lui poniti la ſe
de et la ſperanza uoſtra:acio chel dimonio con ſoi inganni non ui poſſa
pigliare con la diſordinata paura dela morte: ma con deſiderio uogliate
tornare al fine uoſtro. Altro non dico.Bagnateui nel ſangue di Chriſto
crocifixo.Benedicete la fanciulla in Chriſto dolce Ieſu . Ricomandati
me a monna Niera et a Nicolo:et diciteli che ſappiano furare il tempo:
et ſpenderlo con uero et ſancto deſiderio mentre che lhanno.permanete
nela ſancta et dolce dilectione de Dio.Ieſu dolce:Ieſu amore.

ANeri di Landoccio eſſendo eſſo i Piſa quádo ella il mádo al ſcó pře.
Al nome de Ieſu xpo crocifixo et di Maria dolce.   Epiſt.ccclxi.

Te dilectiſſimo et cariſſimo figliolo in Chriſto dolce Ieſu:
Io Catharina ſerua et ſchiaua de ſerui de Ieſu Chriſto:ſcriuo
nel pretioſo ſangue ſuo:con deſiderio di uederti transforma
to nel foco de lardentiſſima charita:ſi che tu ſia uno uaſcello
di dilectione a portare il nome dela parola de dio con myſterii grandi ſoi
nela preſentia del noſtro dolce xpo in terra:et facci fructo có accendere
il deſiderio ſuo: et po io uoglio figliolo mio che apri locchio del cogno
ſcimento nelo obiecto di Chriſto crocifixo:per che eglie quella fonte do
ue ſinnebria lanima trahédone dolci et amoroſi deſiderii: i quali uoglio
che tu diſtendi ſopra il corpo dela ſancta chieſia per honore de dio & ſa

:.λαμβαίων δὲ παρα` ἰ αρύονβς σω,
ὺ κείσιν σου κεινῶ· καὶ ἐπὺ ρὺς ἱούι
ὺ φάγονται οἱ θλίψαντίς σε πὰς σ
ὺ πίωνται, ὡς οἶνον νέον τὸ αἶμα αὐ·
ίσεται πᾶσα σὰρξ, ὅτι ἐπὼ κς̄ ὁ ῥυ
τι λαμβανόμενος ἰ αρύος ἰ ἄκώβ· οὔ τα
ίον τ̄ το βιβλίον, τῶ ἀγρτασίου τῆς
πέςαλα αὐτῆ. ἢ τίνι ὑπρχρέω τ̄ περι
ραηα ὑμᾶς αὐφ̄ · ἰ ἀλὰ τ̄ ἁμρτίαις ὑ,
παῖς ἀνομίαις ὑμῶν· ὑξ α πέςαλα πι
σαρκὶ ἀλό τι ἦλθον ἠ ἒκ ἦν ανος· ἐκς
ἰ πακούων· μὴ, οὐ κ ἰ αρύι ἠ χείρ μου τ
ύω τῶ ὑξελέαθαι, ἰ ἀλὰ τῶ ἐλεσμῶ μ
ὺ θάλασαν· ἠ θήσω ποταμοὺς ὀβρί
ίβνται, οἱ ἰ χθὺες αὐτῶν, απὸ τῶ μὴ
θανῶντωι ἀν δίψει· ἀνδύσω τ̄ ὀρανὸ
΄κκον θύπω δ̄ πρι βόλαιον αὐτῶ. η
ιῶσαν παιδείας, τ̄ γνῶναι ἠνίηα ἀ

PLATE XXII.   Aldus Manutius.   Greek Bible (Haebler,
Incunabula Leaves), 1509.   p. 261

Act IV. Scene 1. A room in the castle. Enter King, Queen, Rosencrantz, and Guildenstern.

King T H E R E'S matter in these sighs, these profound heaves: you must translate: 'tis fit we understand them. Where is your son?

Queen Bestow this place on us a little while.

Exeunt Rosencrantz and Guildenstern.

Ah, mine own lord, what have I seen to-night!

PLATE XXIII. Eric Gill. "I am set naked on your king-dom." <u>Hamlet</u>. Limited Editions Club, 1933, p. 96-97.

The Gospel according to
ST. MARK

T H E beginning of the gospel of Jesus Christ, the son of God;
As it is written in the prophets,
'Behold, I send my messenger before thy face,
Which shall prepare thy way before thee.
The voice of one crying in the wilderness,
Prepare ye the way of the Lord,
Make his paths straight'.
John did baptize in the wilderness, and preach the baptism of repentance for the remission of sins. And there went out unto him all the land of Judæa, and they of Jerusalem, and were all baptized of him in the river of Jordan, confessing their sins. And John was clothed with camel's hair, and with a girdle of a skin about his loins; and he did eat locusts and wild honey; and preached, saying, There cometh one mightier than I after me, the latchet of whose shoes I am not worthy to stoop down and unloose. I indeed have baptized you with water; but he shall baptize you with the Holy Ghost.

And it came to pass in those days, that Jesus came from Nazareth of Galilee, and was baptized of John in Jordan. And straightway coming up out of the water, he saw the heavens opened, and the Spirit like a dove descending upon him.

And there came a voice from heaven, saying, Thou art my beloved Son, in whom I am well pleased.

And immediately the spirit driveth him into the wilder-

PLATE XXIV.   Eric Gill.   The Aldine Bible.   J. M. Dent and Sons, Ltd. , 1934-1936.   vol. 1, p. 90-91.

78

S O oft have I invok'd thee for my Muse,

And found such faire assistance in my verse,

As every Alien pen hath got my use,

And under thee their poesie disperse.

Thine eyes, that taught the dumbe on high to sing,

And heavie ignorance aloft to flie,

Have added fethers to the learneds wing,

And given grace a double Majestie.

Yet be most proud of that which I compile,

Whose influence is thine, and borne of thee,

In others workes thou doost but mend the stile,

And Arts with thy sweete graces graced be.

But thou art all my art, and doost advance

As high as learning, my rude ignorance.

PLATE XXV. Hague and Gill. The Sonnets of William Shakespeare. Cassell and Company, Ltd., 1933. p. 78.

type. Gill says, in An Essay on Typography (p. 38, facing
plate XXVII), "... the style of letter called italic still pre-
serves its cursive character. Most italic types, however
(see fig. 11 #5, plate XXVII), are too sloping and too cursive. There is a great need for a narrower and less sloping
letter which while giving emphasis and difference shall be of
the same non-cursive character as the upright letters they
are used with. Both of the Perpetua and the Joanna italics
(fig. 11 #3, 4, plate XXVII) are so designed."[9] Note plate
XXIV, an example of Gill designing with his own italic forms.
The relationship between the italic and the Roman capitals
interspersed is not a disturbing thing but one wonders if the
degree of emphasis desired is attained? In a normal para-
graph with one or two words in italic (old style) where emphasis is necessary in the text, the attention of the reader is
caught immediately by the change in slant. With as slight a
difference as exists between Joanna Roman and Joanna italic
one doubts the value of setting words apart in this manner.
Would the ordinary reader be impressed or would he, un-
noticing, pass by words so marked? The latter seems evident in plate XXVI, taken from the notes appended to The
Aldine Bible.

Later in the essay Gill says of Greek: "... the same
cursive quality as affects italic has always affected Greek
types (fig. 11 #7, plate XXVII). For some reason or other,
probably the rarity of Greek printing, the leaders of typographic design in the fifteenth century never achieved for
Greek what they did for Latin and the modern languages ...
Many Greek types exist but for the most part they are more
italic than italic."[10] That is to say, they are more cursive
in character and less adapted to typography. Gill designed
(cont'd on p. 68)

Ch. 19

53.13 omit and whoso marrieth her which is put away
doth commit adultery
'whosoever shall put away his wife, except
it be for fornication, and shall marry another,
committeth adultery. * His disciples say'

53.30 omit Good
'And, behold, one came and said unto him,
* Master, what good thing shall I do?'

54.1 for Why callest thou me good? there is none good
but one, that is, God: read:
'Why askest thou me concerning that which is good?
There is One who is good, but if thou wilt enter
into life, keep the commandments'

54.17 a rich man shall hardly i.e. it is hard for a rich man
'it is hard for a rich man to enter into the king-
dom of heaven'

55.2 omit or wife
'And every one that hath forsaken houses, or
brethren, or sisters, or father, or mother, * or
children, or lands, for my name's sake, shall
receive an hundredfold'

55.4 eternal not everlasting but outside or beyond time
'shall inherit life beyond time'

Ch. 20

55.19 omit and whatsoever is right, that shall ye receive
'He saith unto them, Go ye also into the vine-
yard * . So when even was come'

56.6 evil i.e. grudging : good i.e. liberal
'Is thine eye grudging, because I am liberal?'

56.7 omit for many be called, but few chosen

PLATE XXVI. Eric Gill. Notes: St. Matthew. The Aldine
Bible, 1936, p. 150.

typographic design in the fifteenth century never
achieved for Greek what they did for Latin & modern languages. That the thing is possible is shown

ABCDEFGHIJKLMNOPQRSTUVWXYZ
abcdefghijklmnopqrstuvwxyz
abcdefghijklmnopqrstuvwxyz
abcdefghijklmnopqrstuvwxyz

abcdefghijklmnopqrstuvwxyz

ΑΒΓΔΕΖΗΘΙΚΛΜΝΞΟΠΡΣΤΥΦΧΨΩ
αβγδεζηθικλμνξοπρσςτυφχψω
ΑΒΓΔΕΖΗΘΙΚΛΜΝΞΟΠΡΣΤΥΦΧΨΩ
αβγδεζηθικλμνξοπρσςτυφχψω

(Figure 11 : 1 and 2, Perpetua Roman capitals and lower-
case; 3, Perpetua italic; 4, Joanna italic; 5, Caslon Old Face
italic; 6 & 7, Porson Greek capitals & lower-case; 8 & 9,
Perpetua Greek capitals and lower-case.)

by what the Emperor Peter the Great did in the case
of Russian writing. The Russian alphabet is closely
related to the Greek. The formalisation of Russian
script was achieved very successfully by the Dutch
typographers employed by Peter the Great; & the
same thing could be done for Greek. ¶ Many vari-
eties of Greek types exist, but for the most part they
are more italic than the Italics. In recent years at-

Aldus Manutius
Catherina Siena
Epistolae Ed Orazioni
Haebler

Eric Gill
Hamlet

Aldus Manutius
Ibid.

Plate XXVIII.

Inter-linear Study

Eric Gill
Hamlet

Eric Gill
The Aldine Bible

Aldus Manutius
Greek Bible

Eric Gill
Greek specimen - Joanna
p. 39, Essay on Typography

te al loco de ripoſo : & ala uera cita di Hieruſalem.i.uiſion di pace: doue
ogni bene e remunerato:cio e ogni patiétia et bona operatione : la quale
noi adoperiamo in queſta uita. O quáto ſeria matto & ſtolto quello mer

Qu^{een} Bestow this place on us a little while.
Exeunt Rosencrantz and Guildenstern.
Ah, mine own lord, what have I seen to-night!

ſo:& ello p timore dela pena el ſoteraſſe ſotto la terra.ſerrebbe p certo de-
gno di grande reprehenſione & che li fuſſe tolta la uita. Noi ſiamo quel-
li mercadanti a cui e commeſſo el theſoro del tempo con lo libero arbi-

Act IV. Scene 1. A room in the castle. Enter King,
Queen, Rosencrantz, and Guildenstern.

Jerusalem, and were all baptized of him in the river of
Jordan, confessing their sins. And John was clothed with
camel's hair, and with a girdle of a skin about his loins;

ːλαμβαύων δὲ παρα᾽ἰ χύον῾ζς σω,
ὺ κεί σιν σου κεινῶ·καὶ ἐτὼ ῥὺς ἰ̓ού;
ὶ φάϳονται οἱ θλί ψαντίς σε πὰς σ

ΑΒΓΔΕΖΗΘΙΚΛΜΝΞΟΠΡΣΤΥΦΧΨΩ
αβγδεζηθικλμνξοπρσστυφχψω

two Greek fonts with the sole aim of creating Greek capitals
related to Roman capitals, and Greek lower-case letters related to Roman lower-case letters, all within the same family. "The letter and serif form," he said, "is uniform
throughout."[11]

Comparing the Aldine Greek with Gill's design (plates
XXII and XXVII), one can get a clear idea of the basic tradition and of the complete renovation that it underwent in Perpetua and in Joanna Greek. This last named type was used
in the Latin-Greek edition of The Aldine New Testament edited
by Walter Shewring and designed by Gill.[12] It is a singularly
clear and brilliant type.

The Joanna types, Greek, italic and Roman, are based
on traditional types exemplified by the plates shown herein.
Yet their foundation bears the same relationship to tradition
that a grand-aunt might bear her grand-niece by marriage,
one very far removed and without real blood alliance. Although nearly every single letter is identical in form (plate
XXVIII, letters a, e, i, o, m, w, g, l, t, ad infinitum) there is a
decided difference in spirit and in weight. The Gill letters
are taller and narrower (Greek alone excepted) and with much
finer faces. In Greek, however, the converse is true. Gill's
are heavier and clearer than traditional Greek fonts, with no
cursive quality but with the same dignity.

Two names steeped in typographic tradition must be
considered next: John Baskerville and William Caslon.
Though, speaking chronologically, they both belong to the
eighteenth century, Caslon is as much a part of twentieth-
century tradition as of his own. Therefore a discussion of
his work will be reserved for the end of this chapter.

Baskerville aimed to produce a type that would embody

SCENE VI.

GARCIA, ALONZO, GONSALEZ *bloody.*

GONSALEZ.

PERDITION choke your Clamors——
    whence this Rudenefs?
Garcia!

GARCIA.

Perdition, Slavery, and Death,
Are entering now our Doors. Where is the King?
What means this Blood? and why this Face of
    Horror?

GONSALEZ.

No Matter—give me firft to know the Caufe
Of thefe your rafh and ill-tim'd Exclamations.

GARCIA.

The Eaftern Gate is to the Foe betray'd,
Who, but for Heaps of flain that choke the Paf-
    fage,
Had enter'd long ere now, and born down all
Before 'em, to the Palace Walls. Unlefs
The King in Perfon animate our Men,

I 4   *Granada's*

PLATE XXIX. John Baskerville. Page from <u>The Poems</u>
and Plays of William Congreve.

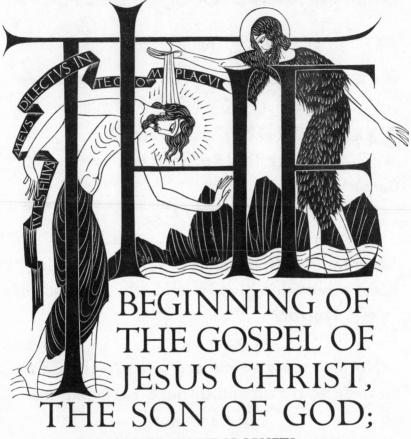

BEGINNING OF THE GOSPEL OF JESUS CHRIST, THE SON OF GOD;

AS IT IS WRITTEN IN THE PROPHETS,
Behold, I send my messenger before thy face,
Which shall prepare thy way before thee.
The voice of one crying in the wilderness,
Prepare ye the way of the Lord,
Make his paths straight.

PLATE XXX.   Eric Gill.   The Baptism of Jesus.   The Four Gospels.   Golden Cockerel Press, 1931, p. 81.

his conception of due proportion. In the <u>Cambridge Bible</u>
(plate XXIX) one sees type that is lighter, more delicate in
form, and with that, made up of less closely related letters
than any of the traditional faces viewed previously. The
balance of thick and thin strokes is really, however, in due
proportion; is a delightful irregularity that itself binds them
together as a closely knit whole. Grace is lacking but not
rhythm. A great deal of light fills the designed page but in
the over-all picture there is enough weight to counter-balance
it. Baskerville was an innovator in his own century of hot-
pressed paper, wove paper, unusual inks, stark type and
light-filled pages. In a word, he was a modern eighteenth-
century printer, whose work became a tradition.

Eric Gill created a type design for, and bearing the
name of, the Golden Cockerel Press which is similar to the
Roman type of Baskerville in form (plate XXX). In fact,
many of the letters are exactly alike. Note the closed head
on the "e," the small body on the "a," the full body of the
"p," "b," "d," "h," and "k," as well as the prolonged "c."
Note, too, the slight difference in the "o" (Gill swings the
thickening down on the left and diagonally up on the right)
and measure the enlarged heads on the "s" and on the "f."
The capitals of Golden Cockerel are monumental in form,
clear-cut, with heavier serifs than Gill usually employs. Of
all of the Gill type-faces this one is most nearly traditional
in form and to a certain extent, in effect. But there is a
saving awkwardness that produces its own individuality, an
earthiness completely devoid of sophistication. Golden
Cockerel type is that type of Gill the creator which digs
deepest into his own personality. From beginning to end,
Gill fought the sophisticated "art world," of which he had
(cont'd on p. 75)

John Baskerville
The Poems and Plays
of William Congreve

Eric Gill
The Four Gospels

Plate XXXI

Inter-linear Study

John Baskerville
The Poems and Plays
of William Congreve

Eric Gill
The Four Gospels

GARCIA.

The Eastern Gate is to the Foe betray'd,
Who, but for Heaps of slain that choke the Paſ-

FORASMUCH AS MANY HAVE TAKEN IN HAND TO SET FORTH IN ORDER A DECLARATION OF THOSE THINGS WHICH ARE MOST SURELY BE-LIEVED AMONG US, EVEN AS THEY DELIVERED them unto us, which from the beginning were eyewitnesses, and ministers of the word; It seemed good to me also, having had perfect understanding of all things from the very first, to write unto thee in order, most excellent Theophilus, That thou mightest know the certainty of those things, wherein thou hast been instructed.

PERDITION choke your Clamors——
whence this Rudeneſs?
Garcia!

THE KING OF JUDÆA, A CERTAIN PRIEST NAMED ZACHARIAS, OF THE COURSE OF ABIA: AND HIS WIFE WAS OF THE DAUGHTERS OF Aaron, and her name was Elisabeth. And they were both righteous before God, walking in all the commandments and

GLUE AND LACQUER

FOUR CAUTIONARY TALES
TRANSLATED FROM THE CHINESE BY
HAROLD ACTON & LEE YI-HSIEH

PREFACE BY
ARTHUR WALEY

With Illustrations from Drawings by
ERIC GILL
interpreted on copper by
Denis Tegetmeier

THE GOLDEN COCKEREL PRESS

PLATE XXXII.   Eric Gill.   Title page.   Glue and Lacquer.
Golden Cockerel Press, 1941.

had a slight taste.   He was well known as a revolutionary.
These facts and his complete humanness are quite evident in
his Autobiography.   Golden Cockerel reflects Gill himself. [13]

The last traditionalist to be mentioned, William Caslon, created fonts of such lasting character that today one
can scarcely examine a shelf of books without encountering
the face of Caslon, old style.   It is on every side of the
publishing world, an eighteenth-century type that is a twentieth-century tradition.   Perhaps this has come about because Caslon has a satisfying quality of interest due to its
delicately perfect modeling.   It has become as comfortable
as an old shoe in the mechanized business of modern printing, and just as common.

Gill created still another type that partakes of the
traditional.   He called it Perpetua.   One finds in it the incisive beauty of the Trajan Column, the interrelation of let-
ter-to-letter found in Jenson, and the delicate modeling of
Caslon (plate XXXII).   Certainly, it is a composite type, but
compare it with each traditional plate mentioned (plate XXXI)
as to form and as to spirit.   Even a cursory glance shows
that an analysis of this particular type fits it more accurately
into the following chapter, which considers the contemporary
forces in Gill design rather than the historical setting of the
Gill types (plate XXXIII).

Notes

1.   Edward Johnson.   Manuscript and Inscription Letters,
        with five plates by A. E. R. Gill.   London: John
        Hogg, 1909.   Pl. 11, 12, 13, 14, and 16.

2.   Edward Johnson.   Ibid.   Pl. 12.

3.   The Book of Kells.

(cont'd on p. 78)

Eric Gill
The Passion of Perpetua
and Felicity

William Caslon
Specimen

Eric Gill
The Passion of Perpetua
and Felicity

Plate XXXIII

Inter-linear Study

William Caslon
Specimen

Eric Gill
Perpetua Roman
An Essay on Typography, p. 39

William Caslon
Specimen - italic

Eric Gill - Ibid.
Specimen - italic

PERPETUA AND

Quousque tand-

O most valiant and blessed martyrs! O truly called and elected unto
the glory of Our Lord Jesus Christ! Which glory he that magnifies,
honours, and adores, ought to read these witnesses likewise, as
being no less than the old, unto the Church's edification; that these
new wonders also may testify that one and the same Holy Spirit
works ever until now, and with Him God the Father Almighty,
and His Son Jesus Christ Our Lord, to Whom is glory and power
unending for ever and ever

AMEN

4

tua consilia non sentis ? constrictam jam
omnium horum conscientia teneri con-
jurationem tuam non vides? quid prox-
ima, quid superiore, nocte egeris, ubi
ABCDEFGHIJKLMNOPQRS
1234567890

5

ABCDEFGHIJKLMNOPQRSTUVWXYZ
abcdefghijklmnopqrstuvwxyz

6   7

vultusque moverunt ?   *abcdefghijklmnopqrstuvwxyz*

4. Eric Gill: Twentieth Century Book Designer. Chap-
        ter I.

5. Ibid.

6. Konrad Haebler. Incunabula Leaves: Traced by Kon-
        rad Haebler. Munich: Weiss and Company, 1927.
        Text-German edition. p. 5.

7. Evan Gill. Bibliography of Eric Gill. London: Cassell
        and Company, Ltd. , 1953. 224p.

8. The Sonnets of William Shakespeare. London: Cassell
        and Company, Ltd. , 1933. p. 156.

9. Eric Gill. An Essay on Typography. p. 38.

10. Eric Gill. , op. cit. , p. 39.

11. Ibid. , p. 40.

12. The Greek edition never got beyond specimen sheets.
        Walter Shewring wrote that this book was not
        published.

13. Eric Gill. Autobiography. New York: Devin-Adair,
        1941. 300p.

CHAPTER 5

CONTEMPORARY CHARACTERISTICS
IN GILL BOOK DESIGNS

"Contemporary book design is the design peculiar to its own age. In this age its designs are marked by: 1) allusive typography, 2) function, 3) simplicity, and 4) a few adventurous new forms. Book design is contemporary only if it has 5) a living fiber of organic growth as its basic quality."[1] This definition will serve as a measure of the contemporary forces to be traced in this chapter.

The force of tradition in seven book designs and four type creations has been considered so far: namely (the books) A Sentimental Journey, The Holy Sonnets, Hamlet, The Aldine Bible (both English and Latin-Greek editions), The Four Gospels, and The Passion of Perpetua and Felicity, and (the types) Bunyan, Joanna--Roman, italic and Greek-- Golden Cockerel, and Perpetua Roman and italic. Concerning these same designs the following questions arise. Are they modern in design? In the contemporary idiom, are the types allusive? Are they functional? Simple? Are there any new forms? Does some vibrant spark in the design reach beyond the surface of the page to reality, or does one discern only the dying quality of ephemera?

One must weigh each book as evidence and, since the type was created in the reverse order of the previous consideration, it would be best to take both lists inversely now.

The Passion of Perpetua and Felicity

The Passion of Perpetua and Felicity is designed in a manner exquisitely modern. It is a book personifying two worlds: one, that of the Roman martyrs; the other, the world of the twentieth century.

Note the allusive typography--that is, type that fits the mood of the text (plate XXXIV). See how on this page Perpetua type combines precision-cut capitals of Roman strength with perfectly balanced lower-case letters in a starkly beautiful face. In this simplicity of form no unnecessary adornment appears. Hair-line serifs are quite apparently an integral part of the balance and harmony which creates a visual rhythm. Note the line of type immediately beneath the martyr. Note the last line.

The pattern of the whole book is as simple as the pattern of this single page. It is functional; that is, fittingly designed to be read freely, easily, with pleasure. There are no barriers to perception and no page seems dead. There is a movement between images, even on this single page, that creates a dynamic dualism, a unity of opposites. (Note the flowing blood on the martyr, the contrapuntal effect of the drapery, the unresolved tension of both figures in the wood engraving.) Each illustration is like a kind of printer's flower, and, like the one on this plate, grows out of the text, being at the same time imperceptibly related to the type and to the page. The whole book, like this particular example, is organically alive with harmonic force.

he was a novice), herself set it upon her own neck. Perchance so
great a woman could not else have been slain (being feared of the
unclean spirit), had she not herself so willed it.

O most valiant and blessed martyrs! O truly called and elected unto
the glory of Our Lord Jesus Christ! Which glory he that magnifies,
honours, and adores, ought to read these witnesses likewise, as
being no less than the old, unto the Church's edification; that these
new wonders also may testify that one and the same Holy Spirit
works ever until now, and with Him God the Father Almighty,
and His Son Jesus Christ Our Lord, to Whom is glory and power
unending for ever and ever

AMEN

PLATE XXXIV.   Eric Gill.   The Martyrdom of St. Saturns.
The Passion of Perpetua and Felicity.   Douglas Cleverdon,
ed.   1932.   p. 29.

Thus the contemporary strains in this design stand
aligned: vibrant beauty, functional simplicity and allusive
typography. This book, designed by Gill, found to be based
on traditional forms, is here seen to be creatively modern,
built with new and beautiful forms in Perpetua type.

The Four Gospels

The full effect of <u>The Four Gospels</u> as a design is
paradoxical: a book that is modern in quality but which remains traditional in pattern (plate XXXV).

One sees much that is above and beyond the surface
of the page, not alone because of the inspired text but also
because of the design as a whole. Each of its parts is so
interlaced that in illustration, titles, capitals, type, layout,
ground, figure and pattern, the imagination and the emotions
are enmeshed in a web of awkward loveliness that produces
sheer pleasure in the viewer.

"Pleasure," Gill says, "is that quality of the mind
that comes from really knowing goodness, truth and beauty."[2]

It is evident from the subtle power of this book design
that the creator had in mind all of the pages of such a book,
all of the words of such a page, all of the letters of such
words, together with their relationships, when he created the
type itself. There is nothing indecisive about Golden Cockerel type. (Note the strong stems, the firm serifs, the human quality of the letter designs. They are far from being
mechanically perfect. It is variations such as those in the
"f," "p," "y" and "g" that bespeak this humanness.)

The illustrations and letters of introduction done by
Gill on wood blocks and used on sixty-four pages control the

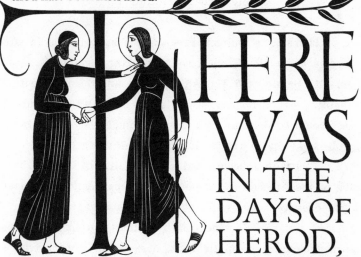

ORASMUCH AS MANY HAVE TAKEN IN HAND
TO SET FORTH IN ORDER A DECLARATION OF
THOSE THINGS WHICH ARE MOST SURELY BE-
LIEVED AMONG US, EVEN AS THEY DELIVERED
them unto us, which from the beginning were eyewitnesses,
and ministers of the word; It seemed good to me also, having
had perfect understanding of all things from the very first,
to write unto thee in order, most excellent Theophilus, That
thou mightest know the certainty of those things, wherein
thou hast been instructed.

HERE
WAS
IN THE
DAYS OF
HEROD,
THE KING OF JUDÆA, A CERTAIN
PRIEST NAMED ZACHARIAS, OF THE COURSE OF
ABIA: AND HIS WIFE WAS OF THE DAUGHTERS OF
Aaron, and her name was Elisabeth. And they were both
righteous before God, walking in all the commandments and

131

PLATE XXXV. Eric Gill. The Visitation. The Four Gospels. Golden Cockerel Press, 1931, p. 131.

lay-out design in such a way that while Gill himself was not
the compositor nor the printer, he was most definitely the
designer of the book (see plates XXX and XXV). The illustrations and the capitals actually govern the type and the text.

    The contemporary quality of this book lies in a design
that is vibrant. (Note the inner radiance of these plates;
and it is as much an integral part of every page as it is of
these two.) The Four Gospels is a creative achievement
that is truly modern.

<h3 style="text-align:center">Hamlet and The Aldine Bible</h3>

    There is a contemporary quality in form and in effect
that sets apart all of the books printed at Pigotts but, of
them all, Hamlet and The Aldine Bible are the most outstanding. Bruce Rogers says, in his book Pi, "a beautiful
book should first be an efficient instrument, it should be
legible and easy to read. It may at the same time be a
work of art with a beauty and a personality of its own. "[3]
Each of these books has a personality apparent to the most
casual observer, or critic: "Eric Gill's press at Pigotts
produced a Hamlet for the Club (Limited Editions), perhaps
the most actually dramatic version extant in modern typography. Mr. Gill set the text in his own Joanna, adding
wood-block initials and illustrations of a strikingly spare and
sinewy kind. This is not mere decoration: it is the sympa-
thetic probing into the play and at the same time a sensitive
adjustment of the gravure's line to the weight of the type. "[4]
(Plates XXXVI and XXXVII.) The exquisite consonance, radiance, and harmony throughout both designs is not marred
in any element--binding, illustration, type of lay-out. The

Act IV. Scene 1. A room in the castle. Enter King,
Queen, Rosencrantz, and Guildenstern.

King   THERE'S matter in these sighs,
these profound heaves:
you must translate:
'tis fit we understand them.
Where is your son?

Qu^{een} Bestow this place on us a little while.

      Exeunt Rosencrantz and Guildenstern.

Ah, mine own lord, what have I seen to-night!

96

The Gospel according to

ST. MARK

T H E beginning of the gospel of Jesus Christ, the son
of God;
As it is written in the prophets,
'Behold, I send my messenger before thy face,
Which shall prepare thy way before thee.
The voice of one crying in the wilderness,
Prepare ye the way of the Lord,
Make his paths straight'.
John did baptize in the wilderness, and preach the baptism of repentance for the remission of sins. And there
went out unto him all the land of Judæa, and they of
Jerusalem, and were all baptized of him in the river of
Jordan, confessing their sins. And John was clothed with
camel's hair, and with a girdle of a skin about his loins;
and he did eat locusts and wild honey; and preached,
saying, There cometh one mightier than I after me, the
latchet of whose shoes I am not worthy to stoop down
and unloose. I indeed have baptized you with water; but
he shall baptize you with the Holy Ghost.

And it came to pass in those days, that Jesus came from
Nazareth of Galilee, and was baptized of John in Jordan.
And straightway coming up out of the water, he saw the
heavens opened, and the Spirit like a dove descending
upon him.

And there came a voice from heaven, saying, Thou art
my beloved Son, in whom I am well pleased.

And immediately the spirit driveth him into the wilder-

91

PLATE XXXVII.   Eric Gill.   The Gospel According to St.
Mark.   The Aldine Bible.   J. M. Dent and Sons, Ltd.,
1934-1936, p. 90-91.

obscure thinness and abtruse thickness which are features of
modern Roman type gone modernistic are not perceptible here.
Even the finest hair-lines are easily seen in any part of either book.   (Some of the photocopy work done from Hamlet
loses the fine lines and distorts the "a's" and the "e's. " This
is only in duplication and not in the original.   Note the capital "E, " "M" and "K, " the "S" and the "G" of plate XXXVI.)

Nor do the new forms found in the type itself detract
from the whole, save perhaps in the italic, which is not quite
italic enough (see plates XXVI and XXXVI).   In spite of this
exception, the end results have proved to be simple, functional, designedly beautiful books.

A Sentimental Journey and The Holy Sonnets

While the lay-out patterns for these two books are
completely different, they are grouped together here because
they make use of the same type as a modern setting for
classic texts.   Bruce Rogers gave his evaluation of Jenson
Roman (the basic traditional type found to be behind this
Bunyan type) in the following quotation: "After twelve years
study of it, minute comparisons with almost every other
Roman letter, ancient and modern, and two or three unsuc-
cessful attempts to reproduce its form in modern matrices,
I believe it to be, at once, the most beautiful and the most
legible type in the world.   Modification of it there may properly be for special purposes, and for modern readers some
alteration of set and alignment may be desirable;   but in
variety and refinement of form and in noble proportion, im-
provement of it is forever impossible. "[5]   The evidence has
shown Bunyan type to be very similar to Jenson type.[6]

XIV

BATTER my heart, three person'd God; for, you

As yet but knocke, breathe, shine, and seeke to mend;

That I may rise, and stand, o'erthrow mee,'and bend

Your force, to breake, blowe, burn and make me new.

I, like an usurpt towne, to'another due,

Labour to'admit you, but Oh, to no end,

Reason your viceroy in mee, mee should defend,

But is captiv'd, and proves weake or untrue.

Yet dearely'I love you,'and would be loved faine,

But am betroth'd unto your enemie:

Divorce mee,'untie, or breake that knot againe,

Take mee to you, imprison mee, for I

Except you'enthrall mee, never shall be free,

Nor ever chast, except you ravish mee.

PLATE XXXVIII.   Eric Gill.   Death Be Not Proud.   The
Holy Sonnets.   J. M. Dent and Sons, Ltd. , 1938.   Sonnet
XIV.

the sword and the sex together,
convent as in himself.

I feel a damp upon my spirits, a
through Calais, upon inquiring af
dead near three months, and was
to his desire, in a little cemetery b
a strong desire to see where they
little horn box, as I sat by his gra·
head of it, which had no business
forcibly upon my affections, that
weak as a woman; and I beg the v

However, the proportions of Jenson are seen in Bunyan but
with an even greater refinement of form.   This defect, which
reduces variety, is overcome by a delicate rhythm.   (see
plate XXXVIII--note the flow from line to line which unifies
the whole).   The page presents a picture of light and harmony that is unique.

Both books (A Sentimental Journey and The Holy Sonnets) are quite evidently contemporary productions (note
plates XXXVIII and XXXIX) because of their functionalism,
their simplicity and their vibrancy.   Each book is adapted to
ease in reading and handling;   each has a simple set-up;
each projects a personality of its own.   The size of each
provides for the first point, lack of undue ornamentation
takes care of the second point, and the combined wholes,
which are unlike other books, has proven them to be creations alive with a delicate pulsation. [7]

Notes

1.   Eric Gill: Twentieth Century Book Designer.   p. 5-7.

2.   Eric Gill.   Beauty Looks After Herself.   New York:
     Sheed and Ward, 1934.   p. 246.

3.   Bruce Rogers.   Pi: A Hodge Podge of the Letters,
     Papers and Addresses Written During the Last
     Sixty Years.   Cleveland: World Publishing Com-
     pany, 1953.   p. 45.

4.   Paul Stoddard.   "The Limited Edition--A New Influence,"
     Penrose Annual XXXVII: 44-49, 1935.

5.   Bruce Rogers.   Pi.   p. 12-13.

6.   Eric Gill: Twentieth Century Book Designer.   p. 53-54.

7.   Clark Library.   Gill Collection.   A Sentimental Journey
     Colophon.   (Note Plate IX.)   This book is not

listed in the <u>Bibliography</u> by Evan Gill but its
Colophon places it as to time, place and publisher.
It is quite evidently a Gill design.

CHAPTER 6

GILL CONCEPTS OF BOOK DESIGN

A selective survey of Gill's ideas on design must be
composed of threads of thought drawn from his books and
articles on a variety of subjects, and from writings about
him.   The chief source for this purpose is his Essay on
Typography.   In this book, he says: "There are two typog-
raphies as there are two worlds, and apart from God or
profits, the best of the one is mechanical perfection and of
the other, sanctity--the commercial article at its best is
simply, physically serviceable and, per accidens, beautiful
in its efficiency;   the work of art at its best is beautiful in
its very substance and, per accidens, as serviceable as an
article of commerce. "[1] As a typographer Gill, never far
from God and always wed to the necessity of supporting his
family, so designed for industry that he was able to live in
the world of art.   That is, he created with machine production in mind (here one speaks of type), using these creations
as works, or as tools for works of art.   Often they were
works that were both beautiful in their very substance and
serviceable as articles of commerce.   Holbrook Jackson explains further that Gill set out to make a book useful, be-
lieving implicitly that beauty would then take care of itself.[2]
In most instances beauty quite apparently did so (note plates

III, XXXIII and XXXIX--all examples of commercial success
beautiful in substance).

Gill did not conceive his workshop at Pigotts as a private press because the element of self-support made it into
a business, more or less at the whim of demand. Still, the
shops were "the enduring home of craftsmanship established
under physical and spiritual conditions that would make good
work possible."[3] Gill would be the first to say that these
conditions were in "the languishing but indestructible world
of the small shopkeeper, the small workshop ... a world in
which the notion of spare time hardly exists, for the thing
is hardly known and very little desired: a world wherein
work is life and love accomplishes it."[4] And all of this because, as he says, "art is the peculiar and appropriate ac-
tivity of man as the lover of God."[5] Explicitly defining this
work, he believes "art is neither representative of nature
nor symbolical of thought. It is a work, an object with a
value of its own: a thing in which the deliberate skill of the
artist has expressed his own love of being, truth, goodness
and beauty--of God."[6] It is a thing of beauty: "the radiance
that shines from things made as they should be made."[7]
Michael Kirk's thesis on The Esthetics of Gill proves that
Gill's sense of beauty was not an alternative nor an escape
from dogmatic religion. It was an immersion in it.[8]

In another article Gill speaks of the workman apart
from his work when he says, "... it will be thought that
writing as an artist I have no proper respect for other sorts
of work. But it should be noticed that I am not claiming a
special loftiness for a class of special persons, for in a normal society--one, that is to say, composed of responsible
persons, responsible for what they do and what they make--

'the artist is [here Gill quotes Ananda Coomaraswamy] not a special kind of man but every man is a special kind of artist!' "[9] On the next page of the same article Gill affirms that "art is a rhetorical activity--that is easily understood, if we think of books, and dramatic plays, of poetry and music, of pictures and sculptures. "[10]

As a book designer Gill was a special kind of artist because he created, according to his own definition, original forms--"By original forms I mean that quality in the thing made which owes its origin to the workman directly or to the artist and is not either an imitation of something seen nor an idea given to him by another person.... Everything made by free workmen has the quality of original form, that is to say, a form for which the maker is responsible.... The only value of the things in our museums is intrinsic. In shape or color or arrangement there is something about them that is of God, godly. And as God reduced chaos to order, so men in past times have given the quality of order to the things made.... Original form is essentially a matter of order.... It is the shining out of being: it is the thing called beauty. "[11] The evidence of the last two chapters of this work points out that Gill working as a designer of books created original forms--forms for which the maker was completely responsible, radiant forms, things of beauty.

Returning to An Essay on Typography, Gill might have been describing his own new type forms when, on the last page, he wrote: "The beauty that Industrialism properly produces is the beauty of bones; the beauty that radiates from the work of men is the beauty of the living face. "[12]

Notes

1. Eric Gill. <u>An Essay on Typography</u>. p. 71.

2. Holbrook Jackson. <u>The Printing of Books</u>. London: Cassell and Company, Ltd., Chapter X, p. 140-154.

3. <u>Eric Gill Workshops</u>, <u>op</u>. <u>cit</u>., p. 1.

4. <u>Typography</u>, <u>op</u>. <u>cit</u>., p. 16-17.

5. <u>Art and Love</u>, <u>op</u>. <u>cit</u>., p. 5.

6. "Art." <u>Blackfriars</u>, 21:681, Dec. 1940.

7. Eric Gill. "Work and Culture," <u>Sacred and Secular</u>, p. 107.

8. Kirk, <u>op</u>. <u>cit</u>., p. 51.

9. "Art." <u>Blackfriars</u>, <u>op</u>. <u>cit</u>., p. 684.

10. <u>Ibid</u>., p. 688.

11. Eric Gill. <u>Christianity and Art</u>. Shakespeare Head Press, 1928, p. 36-42.

12. Gill. <u>Typography</u>, p. 124.

CHAPTER 7

BOOK DESIGN ANALYSIS

This chapter is divided into two main sections: the first considers the tactile qualities of Gill designs, that is, the size, binding, paper and leafedges; the second is concerned with the actual components of the design patterns, including title pages, lay-outs, chapter headings, running titles, illustrations, type and jackets. The examples used do not constitute a survey but provide some evidence to substantiate a few conclusions.

There is no average size for Gill book designs; it varies from book to book. All but six of the books are less than folio in size and are easily handled, being both light and comfortable. The six large formats are The Canterbury Tales, Troilus and Creseyde, two books of Engravings, The Travels and Sufferings of Brebeuf and The Four Gospels. The purpose of these productions seems to call for the dig-nity and elegance of the folio editions.

Each new page size ties in directly with the lay-out design--from the standard 11 by 8 1/2 of The Passion of Perpetua and Felicity to the 5 1/8 by 4 of The Temple Shakespeare. Clothing Without Cloth and The Lord's Song both have the unusual proportions of 9 by 4 1/2 which creates a double page unit that is square. The Green Ship, A

Sentimental Journey and Glue and Lacquer are bound in proportions of ten to seven.   The point to be made is that each
size is fitted to the text and to the over-all design.

The bindings in Gill designs fall into three groups:
1) those planned with exquisite taste regardless of the sub-
sequent and necessarily high cost of the book;   2) those executed as design complements but within the price bracket of
the discriminating buyer;   and 3) those cheap editions for
readers who cannot afford the nicer binding.   Some of these
last mentioned bindings are in the paperback class but with
a unique design for the wrapper of each.

The general survey of books designed by Gill (in the
third chapter of this work) gives the place of the binding in
each edition, showing the relative cost and suggesting the
added beauty.

Any of the first type of selected bindings are full-
bound in the finest of leathers: for example, the vellum edi-
tion of The Canterbury Tales in niger morocco, The Green
Ship in green levant morocco, the limp black leather of The
Temple Shakespeare, the lovely hand-tooled edition of An
Essay on Typography in Welsh sheepskin, or the Limited
Editions Club's Hamlet in golden pigskin, blind-stamped.

There is a high degree of pleasure attached to handling books whose tactile qualities are so keenly refined that
they create joy by reason of their very texture.   Such a binding enhances a book's personality and can provide a special
setting for each new pattern and form.   Gill must have been
aware of this because none of the bindings are ornate, none
extreme.   His choice fell upon the finest quality, the most
fitting and the simply pleasing bindings.

One feels the value of these same tactile enhancements

in the binding designs of the books in the second class enu-
merated.   These last combine fine leathers and exquisitely
patterned or subtly pleasing boards in quarter bindings, so
that one's sense of touch is stimulated and the outer loveliness of the book becomes a promise of inner beauty.   Examples of these are the bindings of A Sentimental Journey,
Glue and Lacquer and Troilus and Criseyde.

The cheap editions have little to redeem their drab
cloth bindings save clearly marked titles in beautiful lettering
and a few interesting printer's devices.   Comparing cover
titles from book to book, the legibility and incisive beauty of
those done in Gill titling are evident, while the titles on his
miscellaneous press productions are less well-chosen typographically.   Even the Caslon titles suffer by this comparison,
perhaps because of their deadly usualness.

There are two outstanding printer's devices used on
this class of cover; the dog and the tree (Plate V), a Hague
and Gill press mark, and St. Thomas' hands used as an
identifying symbol on books written by Gill.   The latter, with
its variant (a narrow V of about 60 degrees rather than one
with wide flung arms), is also used on the title page of most
books of Gill authorship.   The paperbacks have a design in
each instance that is unique.   Trousers and The Unholy
Trinity are both examples of this interest-rousing quality of
Gill which is not blatant advertising but sensitive interpretation.

Opening one or all of the Gill book designs brings an
awareness of the paper, which also results in both a visual
and a tactile pleasure.   Except some books for miscellaneous
presses, all are printed on paper of the finest quality.   If
not vellum, then one of three kinds of handmade paper

(Batchelor, Basingwerk or Barcham Green, especially watermarked) is used.   The one exception, <u>An Essay on Typog-
raphy</u>, was printed on Arnold's and Foster's Pure Rag paper.
In effect, the first edition of this book did not provoke the
visual and textural joy of the others because the choice of
grey was a mistake.   It seems to swallow the ink and to
soften the precision of the Joanna type.   The second edition
was much improved by switching to a soft white.   The handmade papers, on the other hand, speak of hidden tensility,
tastefulness and harmony.   The ink bites into them, a brilliant figure on a soft tenuous ground.

A word about the leaf-edges in Gill book designs may
be a discordant note.   Wherever the edges were left uncut--
as in <u>Id Quod</u>, <u>The Song of the Soul</u> and <u>Art-Nonsense</u>--the
natural edges of the paper, which in the 'thirties may have
been pleasing, are today so ingrained with dust that they are
not pleasant to touch.   Even when the top edges are cut the
other edges often are not.

One device that adds an interesting design note is the
use of color on the top edges of the cut pages in many instances.   Warm red, deep green, sooty black or gilt, har-
monizing with the case, creates from the first moment of
handling a sense of delight.   In <u>Twenty-five Nudes</u> the use
of black on the top edges also balances the delicate line engravings on each page and adds an aspect of permanence.
The rebellious quality in Gill's character is suggested by the
use of prescient red on the top edges of the <u>Autobiography</u>;
a sense of elegance is built up from the beginning by the use
of gilt top edges in <u>Clothes</u>;   deep green top edges in the
second edition of <u>An Essay on Typography</u> suggest the root
of the matter even before one opens a page.

(cont'd on p. 103)

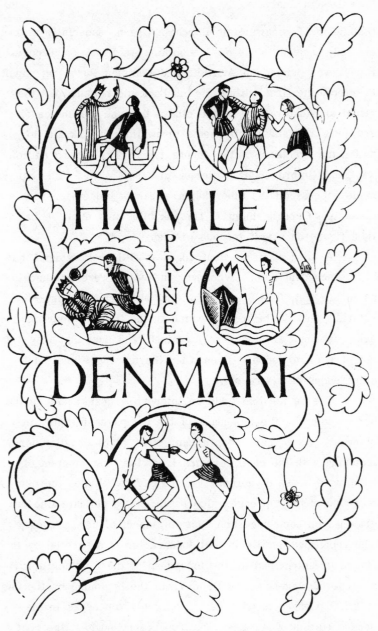

HAMLET
PRINCE OF
DENMARI

PLATE XL. Title page. <u>Hamlet</u>. Limited Editions Club, 1933, Introduction.

ART-NONSENSE
AND OTHER ESSAYS
BY ERIC GILL

LONDON

CASSELL & CO., LTD. & FRANCIS WALTERSON

1929

THE PASSION OF
PERPETUA AND
FELICITY

MARTYRED AT CARTHAGE A.D. CCIII

A NEW TRANSLATION BY

W. H. SHEWRING

WITH ENGRAVINGS ON WOOD

BY

ERIC GILL

London, 1929

PRINTED FOR 'THE FLEURON'

in Perpetua roman made by the

Lanston Monotype Corporation from the design of

ERIC GILL

PLATE XLII.   Title page.   The Passion of Perpetua and Felicity.

Christopher Sandford, in "The Aesthetics of the Illustrated Book," says: "A book cannot be beautiful if one of its features is ugly, nor indeed if one is out of harmony, out of tune, in the wrong key."[1] This harmony, Gill believed, began with the paper. "Paper is to the printer as stone is to the sculptor, one of the raw materials of his trade...."[2] This is logical because on the printing surface depends the crispness of line necessary for fine typography and for fine wood engravings. Thus, the paper itself is a source of good design.

Gill uses the title page as a statement of design, as a sort of prologue to the over-all pattern of layouts. The series of title pages (Sacred and Secular, Money and Morals, The Unholy Trinity, Work and Property, for example) combining the title with the table of contents is a simple, functional and radiantly clear preamble for the pages to come, which are also simple, functional and vitally alive (see Plate IV).

Many of the Gill title pages are unique wood engravings; for example, The Travels and Sufferings of Brebeuf, which utilizes the fact that in a book two facing pages become one unit of visual experience. Here, Gill, by means of multiple blocks, successfully uses the double-page spread as a title page. In The Green Ship, by means of six blocks, he uses the same process to achieve a new effect. The title pages for Troilus and Criseyde, for Phaedo and for Hamlet (plate XL), though quite similar to each other are vitally living designs allusive to the text. The title page of Art-Nonsense is also outstanding design but in the white line block technique (plate XLI). In contrast to this is the delicate wood-engraved title page of Twenty-five Nudes. Other

title pages of Gill design employ vigorous blocks of lettering
and design in patterns to set the pace in intense emotion,
such as those of Passio Domini, The Song of the Soul and
The Temple Shakespeare, or patterns for title pages such as
Quia Amore Langueo and Clothing Without Cloth.

Occasionally Gill uses the special emphasis mark in
lay-out, or a hanging indenture form for paragraphing as
fresh and quite pleasing design props (plates XLIII, XLIV
and XLV).

In The Four Gospels the chapter headings (plate XXX)
are virile designs; in The Sentimental Journey the running
titles have an adhesive quality (plate XVIII).   Clever design
practices are used in the lay-out of each book to bind the
whole in beauty with just the right emphasis.

The over-all lay-out of each book has a structural organization that actually integrates the whole into one harmo-
nious design from the most simply patterned paper-back to
the most complex.   The Unholy Trinity is an example of the
first type and The Four Gospels of the last.   Kepes, in The
Language of Vision, says that structural order is living space
and that printing is living or dead depending upon the organization of its blank spaces.[3]   Gill, in his lay-out designs,
takes the contemporary qualities of precision, simplicity and
forcefulness and adds that "rhythmic organization that becomes spatial progression."[4] (A Sentimental Journey, Plate
XXXIX; The Aldine Bible, Plate XXXVII; The Passion of
Perpetua and Felicity, Plate XXXIV).

The Holy Sonnets are arranged in radiant patterns,
suited to their form: balanced, proportionate, related.   The
Aldine Bible, too, was designed deliberately to be read as
literature, combining graciousness with convenience, providing

(cont'd on p. 108)

better shall not be at the mercy of the worse; how
to ensure that the merely cunning and grasping shall
not reduce their brothers to slavery; how to reduce
the man of money and the controller of credit to
their proper subordination.

¶ And brotherhood is poverty—that is the secret. Revealed
in all religions, and, in spite of countless saints and
prophets, hardly yet known to men.
We think things can be put right by fire and slaughter
or by Act of Parliament, or by revolution.
Because we have failed to win the strong to reason we
proclaim with Mussolini, that 'freedom is a conces-
sion of the state'.
Because wicked men have sequestered to their private
aggrandizement the riches that are designed for the
common good, therefore we say with Karl Marx and
his followers, 'all individual appropriation of the
means of production is evil'.
We forget that man precedes the State and that it is not
the service of men but that of God which is freedom.
We forget that the hireling flieth, because he is a hireling, and not because he is evil—and that individual
appropriation of the means of production is ordained

PLATE XLIII.   Eric Gill.   Sacred and Secular.   J. M. Dent
and Sons, Ltd. , 1939.   p. 54.

I ¶ With good art prudence should have no quarrel;
God gave man senses that man should have
pleasant feelings.
The reasonable pleasure of the senses is the
God-designed reward of those acts, such
as eating and "sleeping," which God wills
men to do.
¶ With good art prudence should have no quarrel;
God gave men minds wherewith to have
pleasant thoughts.
The reasonable pleasure of the mind is the reward of
those acts which are called contempla-
tive: that is to say: the vision of Being,
the vision of things as ends.
But many prudent men quarrel with art, however
good, because many prudent men are
prudes.
The prude is afraid of the pleasure of the
senses.
And many prudent men quarrel with art, however
good, because many prudent men are
proud.
The proud man scorns anything not in imitation of himself: that is to say: he scorns
anything which has not himself for its
end.

28

PLATE XLIV. Eric Gill. <u>Beauty Looks After Herself</u>.
Sheed and Ward, 1933, p. 28.

art is in revolt against Victorian men-
: is its own mentality? Apart from the
iusiasm for objectivity and detestation of
 and representation and anecdotage,
)urse no one binding idea among modern
 v could there be unless they were all
 all Baptists or all Hyperborean mystics?
 perhaps one tendency more noticeable
 and that is the tendency to return to
 d elemental ideas. This is seen in the
 iusiasm for negro sculptures—an en-
 ich reflects, on the higher plane of intel-
 s, what, on the lower plane of physical
 is reflected by jazz music. But the in-
 nitive sculptures is not the only form of
 ainst worn-out sentiment. Any kind of
 ing seems preferable to the dead and by
 ; frowziness of sham Gothic and sham
 nticism. And the elemental is not by
 ie coarse or uncouth or even simple.

PLATE XLV.   Eric Gill.   Beauty Looks After Herself.

both beauty of form and ease of use. It is in this way, says
the Times Literary Supplement critic, that it releases for
the first time the full meaning of the text.

Speaking of The Four Gospels, in 1932, a Times
Literary Supplement critic said: "It would be rash to say
that this is the most beautiful book which even the Golden
Cockerel Press has produced," and then he goes on to tell
of a vain hunt for a jarring note, an unworthy design pattern.
The type he describes as "superb," the wood cuts "intensely
dramatic, even humorous," and "the whole design full of passion balanced by an intensity of restraint."[5]

Still another critic writes of Quia Amore Langueo:
"the lovely edition of the loveliest of Middle English mystical
poems ..." designed with "tenuous depth and tenderness."[6]

It is very difficult in most of the Gill book designs to
consider the illustrations apart from the book design as a
whole because even Gill himself regarded them "as a kind of
printer's flower." In the design of The Canterbury Tales
the illustrations control the text, as do those of The Four
Gospels. "The most admirable unity is achieved between
lettering and illustration. The balance between the two elements is perfect; they exist as it were in a wood-engraved
world, where letters and human figures, having equal reality,
can be grouped without the slightest incongruity"[7] (plates II
and III). In fact, wherever Gill uses illustration it grows
from the text, and the printmaker and the typographer are
one, the same man's unity of purpose, materials, and design
bringing about a definite impact--one created by the unusual
relation between text and picture. Not many of his engravings are units in themselves, as is evident in either book of
Engravings, which separate the illustrations from the text

PLATE XLVI. Eric Gill. A page from <u>The Canterbury</u>
<u>Tales</u>, reproduced from <u>Engravings</u>, Faber and Faber, 1933.
Hague and Gill Press.

PLATE XLVII.   Eric Gill.   Frontispiece for St. John's
Gospel.   The Aldine Bible, p. 90.

in a kind of catalog.   One sees that the patterns of which
they are a part, which they balance or complement, are
necessary to their perfect accomplishment (plates XLVI and
XLVII).

A TLS critic, speaking of The Aldine Bible in 1936,
remarks that to illustrate the Bible is a work of superfluity,
but in this instance "its prints are properly decorous, illus-
trative allusion, architectural in form"[8] (plates XXXIX and
XLVII).

Two years earlier a TLS critic, reviewing Gill's illustrations, says he is "a designer in highly simplified facts"
whose pictures "are made to seem a natural growth from the
text ... never irrelevant ... never concealing his individuality."[9]   Today's critic would echo this.

Many have called the Gill illustrations "stylized," but
this is not the result of a deliberate adaptation of form to a
particular style;   it is the intense purpose of the artist re-
strained by interpretation to be impersonal.   Gill makes this
quite clear in his Essays, Letters, and Autobiography.   Note
the illustration for The Aldine Bible, The Passion of Perpetua
and Felicity, The Holy Sonnets (plates XXXVII, XXVII and
XXXVIII).   They are designedly disciplined.

Most book designers must build patterns with type
which they have chosen from a more or less limited supply
of available faces.   Gill designed with types that he himself
created, in some cases for a particular book, in some for a
particular press, and always with a definite approach in mind.
Two of the eight chapters of this book, chapters 4 and 5, are
concerned with an analysis of types of his design.   It remains
but to examine his type in the light of the over-all pattern of
his book designs.   Is it legible?   It it allusive?   Is it beautiful?

GILL : BEAUTY LOOKS AFTER HERSELF

look after truth
and goodness...
BEAUTY
LOOKS AFTER
HERSELF
—in these collected papers
ERIC GILL
is concerned with the

PLATE XLVIII. Eric Gill. Book Jacket. Beauty Looks
After Herself.

PLATE XLIX.   Eric Gill.   Book Jacket.   <u>An Essay on</u>
<u>Typography</u>.   Sheed and Ward, 1931.

"I firmly believe," says Fred Goudy, an American authority on typography, in his book Typologia: "that the best type for our use must have letter-forms based on the shape fixed by tradition, fresh expressions into which new life and vigor have been infused, creating new types which are characterized by severe restraint and which exhibit the poise and reposeful quality that are always pleasing."[10] So far we have shown that Gill type designs of the Golden Cockerel, Joanna, Perpetua and Bunyan families have definite traditional bases (Chapter IV), while being at the same time imbued with qualities of evident contemporary force (Chapter V). Excepting the Joanna italic, critics have found these types legible, allusive, and beautiful. Quite specifically they say: "The type used in The Aldine Bible is large, clear and beautiful."[11] "It is Mr. Gill the printer that is evident in the beautiful production printed in the 14 point Bunyan of The Holy Sonnets."[12] "The type is superb" (The Four Gospels).[13] "Perpetua capitals could not be surpassed."[14] The continued use of these type faces in recent book design is an added proof of their fitness and beauty. On page 230 of Gill's Autobiography is appended a list of printing types designed by Gill and the companies that cut the punches for him. It is interesting to note that since Gill's death, all save one of the types which had not then been cut by Monotype have been converted for machine press use. Joanna, the type which Gill named after his youngest daughter and chose as the private face for the press which he established together with her husband, made its debut at the Exhibition (Monotype House, London) in the field for which it had originally been intended, that of the Monotype Machine Corporation.[15] In 1952 Bunyan became a machine type under the new name of

(cont'd on p. 119)

PLATE L.   Eric Gill.   Detail from title page.   <u>Art-</u>
<u>Nonsense</u>.

look after truth
and goodness...

BEAUTY

LOOKS AFTER

HERSELF

PLATE LI.   Gill Sans type.   Beauty Looks After Herself.

_{THE} PERPETUA _{TYPE}

CUT FROM THE DESIGNS MADE BY

ERIC GILL

FOR THE LANSTON MONOTYPE CORPORATION

LONDON

The following founts only have been made to date; it is projected
to cut the usual sizes for book and display work

(13 point)

ABCDEFGHIJKLM NOPQRSTUUVWXYZ &
ABCDEFGHIJKLMNOPQRSTUVWXYZ
abcdefghijklmnopqrstuvwxyyz fi ff fl ffi ffl   1234567890
.,:;!?-''()-""—

(Titling Capitals, 24 point)

ABCDEFGHIJJKLMNO
PQRRSTUUVWXYZ&

(Titling Capitals, 30 point)

ABCDEFGHIJJKL
MNOPQRRSTUU
VWXYZ&

PLATE LII.   Type specimen.   The Fleuron, VII.

PLATE LIII.　Eric Gill.　Title page.　<u>The Passio Domini</u>.
Golden Cockerel Press, 1926.

Pilgrim, cut by Linotype.   Perpetua has had more than
thirty years of use in machine presses.

The Penrose Annual for 1959 carried an article by
Paul Beaujon in which he remarks: "What a deep satisfac-
tion he would have derived from the knowledge that certain
of his types had become part of the very texture of English
life. "[16]   Eric Gill worked better than he knew when he
created fonts fulfilling his dream: "One of the most alluring
enthusiasms that can occupy the mind of the letterer is that
of inventing a really logical and consistent alphabet having
a distinctive sign for every sound. "[17]

This has been evident because Golden Cockerel,
Joanna, Perpetua and Bunyan have individual forms whose
characteristics of balance and true proportion relate the
figures within the families so that they all hand together
when forming words and page designs.   Each has an air of
its own with no affectation of antiquity.   They are functional.
They are simple.   In a word, they are beautiful.

To conclude this analysis, the book jackets (plates
XLVIII and XLIX) designed by Gill were examples of good
advertising technique: simple, functional, and clear.   Occasionally they were dramatic;   most often they were exciting;
always they were well designed.   Gill considered the definite
purpose of each, carefully adapting his forms to this end.

Notes

1.   Christopher Sandford.   "The Aesthetics of the Illus-
          Book," The Dolphin, 2:83.   New York: Limited
          Editions Club, 1955.

2.   Eric Gill.   An Essay on Typography, p. 82.

3.   Gyorgy Kepes.   The Language of Vision.   Chicago:

Paul Theobold, 1949. p. 32.

4. Ibid. , p. 59.

5. Times Literary Supplement. February 18, 1932.
      p. 110.

6. Ibid. , September 4, 1937. p. 949.

7. The Dolphin. New York: The Limited Editions Club,
      1933. p. 352.

8. Times Literary Supplement. January 25, 1936. p. 67.

9. Ibid. , July 26, 1934. p. 525.

10. Fred Goudy. Typologia. Los Angeles: University of
       California Press, 1940. p. 34.

11. Times Literary Supplement. October 10, 1936. p. 801.

12. Ibid. , December 24, 1938. p. 812.

13. Ibid. , February 18, 1932. p. 110.

14. Ibid. , September 27, 1932. p. 704.

15. Paul Beaujon. "The Diuturnity of Eric Gill," Penrose
       Annual, 1959.

16. Ibid.

17. Eric Gill. An Essay on Typography, p. 59.

CHAPTER 8

ERIC GILL: BOOK DESIGNER
A CONCLUSION

Manifold interest in the man, his philosophy, his creative work, and his influence seems to have grown to international proportions since Gill's death in 1940.   The William
Andrews Clark Memorial Library in Los Angeles, where this
study began, has done a great deal to foster this interest.
So, too, have other rare book collectors, bibliographers,
biographers and critics of Gill in the United States, Great
Britain and Europe.   His stone-sculptures, books, and book
designs are in many libraries and museums of note, as well
as in private collections.   While the materials at the Library
of Congress are not as extensive nor as rare in numbered,
signed editions of the fine printing to be found in the above
mentioned library, they are a particularly rich source for
new studies. [1] The Life of Eric Gill written by the late
Robert Speaight is more nearly a synthesis of Gill's work
and character because he had access directly to the Gill papers and materials at Pigotts.   But his purpose was not to
establish Gill as a designer.

It was proposed in Chapter 1 to discover how and to
what extent Eric Gill was influenced by the forces of tradition
to produce new and beautiful forms in book design.   Were
Gill's book designs derivative of the past, or of both the past

121

and the present?   Do his works reflect a modern element?
Was there a personal translation that allowed for the creation of new forms?   Were these forms actually different--
a picture of a contemporary age?   Were they and are they
really beautiful?[2]

All of the evidence of this book proves that Gill's
book designs were derived from traditional designs.   Forces
in printing have been traced from the 4th-century Trajan
Column inscription to Gill's incisive Perpetua Capitals;   from
the 9th-century minuscules of the Book of Kells to the radiantly similar Golden Cockerel type design;   from the delicately pulsating Bunyan back to its traditional prototype,
15th-century Jenson Roman, and the Roman of Sweynheim
and Pannartz.   Further influences of this same century were
discovered stemming from Aldus Manutius' Roman, Greek,
and italic types to Joanna Roman, Greek and italic;   from
Baskerville and Caslon in the 18th century to Gill and his
Perpetua type in the 20th century.   Clearly traditional forms
were discerned influencing these designs.

Contemporary forces in book design were defined as
allusive typography, functional design, simplicity, and the
creation of vital new forms.   The evidence of these characteristics in the study of Gill's mature work as a book designer points up the second conclusion: that Gill's designs
are derivatives of the present as well as of the past.   They
reflect the modern elements of allusive typography, functionalism and simplicity.   There has been a personal translation
and experience into new forms--forms that are beautiful.
The Aldine Bible and Joanna type, The Four Gospels and
Golden Cockerel, The Passion of Perpetua and Felicity and
Perpetua type, and A Sentimental Journey and Bunyan are

proof proper of this, to mention only four examples. The
forms of type are actually different, as witnessed by their
adoption into contemporary tradition.

One point bears heavily upon this conclusion, namely
the picture of this contemporary age as presented by the
Gill designs which, in each instance examined (The Aldine
Bible, Hamlet, The Holy Sonnets, The Four Gospels and A
Sentimental Journey), were simple, functional, and vitally
alive, and which allowed the illustrations to grow out of each
new text and text-design. Thus, the functionalism of the
age extended from the tactile qualities designed for ease and
pleasure into the visual realm of beauty through consonance,
proportion and clarity.

So a strange and penetrating loveliness, like late summer evenings, falls on the lifescape of the Typographer-De-
signer. Work became increasingly difficult for Eric Gill
during the last year of his life. Prolonged rest did not
shake the racking cough and recurring fever that plagued
him. Some of his monument carving had to be deferred as
did his lecturing and some printing. But the manuscript of
the Autobiography, completed between February 28 and
June 1 of that year, received the Literary Award for 1940.
This book was the history of the mental and spiritual growth
of a man sensitive to the point of extremity, sensuous, virile,
dominantly a rebel, yet always quiescent to Divine mandate.

His last two weeks were characteristically interwoven
with plans and with work. The actual drawings for Glue and
Lacquer illustrations were done in the hospital while waiting
for the doctors to operate on his lungs. Here Gill rested,
and wrote, and drew designs. All the while, his deep sense
of God kept him serene but still fighting.

The end, which was so much a beginning, came
quickly.   Accounts of his death and the flowing obituaries
which followed fast upon it do not indicate that last spurt
of effort which must have hurtled him into the presence of
God.   Maritain, speaking generally in his book, The Responsibility of the Artist, affirms of such a man a lifelong
dualism like that which Gill made his own in creative endeavor as an artist/book-designer who also was a "Christian
Revolutionary."   "I have said again and again that Beauty
and Poetry are an inexorable absolute which requires a total
gift of oneself and which suffers no division.   Only with God
can a man give himself twice over at the same time, first
to his God and second to something which is a reflection of
his God."[3]

Gill might have been speaking autobiographically when
in the preface to Engravings he said: "Augustine asked--
'What do I love when I love my God?' and the artist asks--
"What do I desire when I desire Good?'   The first answer
is that as an artist I desire above and before all things
beauty, because the beautiful is above and before all things
desirable, and (quoting here St. Thomas Aquinas) Gill adds,
" 'from the Divine beauty the being of all things is derived!' "[4]

Notes

1.   The plates in the first edition of this book were poor
     because they were made from photocopies rather than
     high-contrast negatives.   For this edition, new copies
     of many illustrations were done, either by the Library
     of Congress Photo Duplicating Department or by the
     author.

2.   Eric Gill: Twentieth Century Book Designer.   p. 3-4.

3.   Jacques Maritain.   The Responsibility of the Artist.

New York: Charles Scribner's and Sons, 1960.
p. 114.

4.   Eric Gill.   <u>Engravings</u>, p. 18.

BIBLIOGRAPHY

PRIMARY SOURCES

Acton, Harold and Yi-hsieh, Lee (tr.). Glue and Lacquer. Waltham St. Lawrence, Berkshire: Golden Cockerel Press, 1941.

Anand, Mulk Raj. The Lost Child. London: J. A. Allen (Hague and Gill Press), 1934.

Attwater, Donald. Cassell's Catholic Encyclopedic Dictionary. London: Cassell and Company, Ltd. , n. d.

Bennett, H. S. , ed. Quia Amore Langueo. London: Faber and Faber (Hague and Gill Press), 1937.

Besterman, Theodore, tr. Travels and Sufferings of Brebeuf. Waltham St. Lawrence, Berkshire: Golden Cockerel Press, 1938.

Chaucer, Geoffrey. The Canterbury Tales, 4 vols. Waltham St. Lawrence, Berkshire: Golden Cockerel Press, 1928-1931.

_____. Troilus and Criseyde. Waltham St. Lawrence, Berkshire: Golden Cockerel Press, 1927.

Clay, Enid. The Constant Mistress. Waltham St. Lawrence, Berkshire: Golden Cockerel Press, 1934.

Coppard, A. E. The Hundreth Story. Waltham St. Lawrence, Berkshire: Golden Cockerel Press, 1931.

Donne, John. The Holy Sonnets. London: J. M. Dent and Sons, Ltd. (Hague and Gill Press), 1938.

Ege, Otto. _Original Leaves from Famous Bibles_. Cleveland: Western Reserve University Press, 1929.

Evans, Henry Herman. _John Baskerville: The Gracious Infidel_ (insert original leaf from _The Poems and Plays of William Congreve_, printer John Baskerville), p. 155.

Fillion, Aloysius, ed. _Passio Domini Nostri Jesu Christi_. Waltham St. Lawrence, Berkshire: Golden Cockerel Press, 1926.

Gill, Eric. _Art and a Changing Civilization_. Twentieth Century Library. London: John Lane, The Bodley Head, 1934.

_____. "Art and Books," _The Book Collector's Quarterly_, X:1-8, April, 1933.

_____. "Art and Love," _Blackfriars_, Oct. 1924.

_____. _Art and Love_. Bristol: D. Cleverdon, 1927.

_____. _Art and Love_. Waltham St. Lawrence, Berkshire: Golden Cockerel Press, 1928.

_____. _Art and Prudence_. Waltham St. Lawrence, Berkshire: Golden Cockerel Press, 1928.

_____. _Art-Nonsense and Other Essays_. London: Cassell and Company Ltd. , 1929.

_____. _Autobiography_. London: Jonathan Cape Ltd. , 1940.

_____. _Autobiography_. New York: Devin-Adair, 1941.

_____. _Autobiography_. London: Jonathan Cape Ltd. , 1949.

_____. _Autobiography_. New York: Biblo and Tannen, 1968.

_____. _Beauty Looks After Herself_. London: Sheed and Ward, 1933.

_____. _Beauty Looks After Herself_. New York: Books for Libraries, 1966. (Essay and General Literature Index Reprint).

_____. Christianity and Art. Stratford-upon-Avon: Francis Walterson, 1927.

_____. Christianity and the Machine Age. New York: Macmillan, 1940.

_____. Clothes. London: J. Cape, 1931.

_____. Clothing Without Cloth: An Essay on the Nude. Waltham St. Lawrence, Berkshire: Golden Cockerel Press, 1931.

_____. "The Criterion in Art," The Dublin Review, 366:63178, July, 1928.

_____. Drawings from Life. London: Hague and Gill Ltd. , 1940.

_____. "Eating Your Cake," The Penrose Annual, XXXIX:17-20, 1937.

_____. Engravings to the Year 1927. Bristol: Douglas Cleverdon, 1929.

_____. Engravings: 1928-1933. London: Faber and Faber (Hague and Gill Press), 1934.

_____. An Essay on Typography. London: Sheed and Ward (Hague and Gill Press), 1931.

_____. An Essay on Typography. 2nd Edition. London: Sheed and Ward (Hague and Gill Press), 1936.

_____. An Essay on Typography. (Reissued) London: Dent and Sons, 1941.

_____. Essays. London: Jonathan Cape Ltd. , 1942.

_____. First Nudes--Sketch Book #1. New York: Citadel Press, 1954.

_____. From the Jerusalem Diary. London: Jonathan Cape Ltd. , 1953.

_____. Id Quod Visum Placet. Waltham St. Lawrence, Berkshire: Golden Cockerel Press, 1926.

130   Eric Gill

_____. In a Strange Land. London: Jonathan Cape Ltd.,
1944.

_____. It All Goes Together. New York, London: Devin-
Adair, 1944.

_____. It All Goes Together. New York: Books for
Libraries, 1971. (Essay and General Literature Index
Reprint).

_____. Last Essays. London: Jonathan Cape Ltd., 1942.

_____. The Lord's Song. Waltham St. Lawrence, Berk-
shire: Golden Cockerel Press, 1934.

_____. Money and Morals. London: Faber and Faber
(Hague and Gill Press), 1934.

_____. The Necessity of Belief. London: Faber and
Faber Ltd., 1936.

_____. "Sacred and Secular." (A lecture) Newport,
Rhode Island: J. Stephens, 1939.

_____. Sacred and Secular. London: J. M. Dent and
Sons, Ltd., (Hague and Gill Press), 1940.

_____. Sculpture and the Living Model. London: Sheed
and Ward (Hague and Gill Press), 1932.

_____. Stations of the Cross. Union Village, New
Jersey: The Sowers Press, 1944.

_____. Trousers. London: Faber and Faber Ltd.
(Hague and Gill Press), 1937.

_____. Twenty-five Nudes. London: J. M. Dent and
Sons, Ltd. (Hague and Gill Press), 1939.

_____. The Unholy Trinity. London: J. M. Dent and
Sons, Ltd. (Hague and Gill Press), 1948.

_____. Wood Engravings. Ditchlings, Sussex: St.
Dominic's Press, 1924.

_____. Work and Leisure. London: Faber and Faber,
Ltd. (Hague and Gill Press), 1935.

_____. Work and Property. London: J. M. Dent and
Sons, Ltd. (Hague and Gill Press), 1937.

Haebler, Konrad. Incunabula: Original Leaves Traced by
Konrad Haebler. Munich: Weiss and Company, 1927.
Vol. 1: German, 110 leaves; Vol. II: Italian, 120
leaves; Vol. III: West European, 60 leaves.

James, M. R., ed. The Aldine Bible. 4 vols. London:
J. M. Dent and Sons, Ltd. (Hague and Gill Press),
1934-1936.

John-of-the-Cross, St. Song of the Soul. Capel-Y-Effin:
Francis Walterson, 1927.

King James Version. The Four Gospels. Waltham St.
Lawrence, Berkshire: Golden Cockerel Press, 1931.

_____. Song of Solomon. (German). Weimar: Cranack
Press, 1931. Leipzig: Von Hans Bardotte, 1967.

Miller, Patrick. The Green Ship. Waltham St. Lawrence,
Berkshire: Golden Cockerel Press, 1936.

Quia Amore Langueo (Middle English Poem). London:
Faber and Faber, 1937.

Shakespeare, William. All of the Love Poems of William
Shakespeare. New York: Citadel Press, 1963.

_____. Hamlet. London: Limited Editions Club (Hague
and Gill Press), 1933.

_____. The New Temple Shakespeare, 40 Vols. London:
J. M. Dent and Sons, Ltd., 1934-1936.

_____. The Sonnets of William Shakespeare. London:
Cassell and Company, Ltd. (Hague and Gill Press),
1933.

Shewring, Walter, ed. The Aldine Bible. Latin-Greek Edition. London: J. M. Dent and Sons, Ltd., n.d.

_____. Letters of Eric Gill. London: Jonathan Cape
Ltd., 1947.

_____. Letters of Eric Gill. New York: Devin-Adair,
1948.

_____, tr. The Passion of Perpetua and Felicity. Bristol: Douglas Cleverdon (Hague and Gill Press), 1932.

_____, tr. The Passion of Perpetua and Felicity, insert in The Fleuron, VII. London: The Fleuron Ltd. (Hague and Gill Press), 1929.

Sterne, Laurence. A Sentimental Journey. London: Limited Editions Club (Hague and Gill Press), 1936.

SECONDARY SOURCES (SELECTED)

Aldis, Harry G. The Printed Book. New York: Macmillan, 1936.

Attwater, Donald. A Cell of Good Living. London: C. Chapman, 1969.

_____. Modern Christian Revolutionaries. New York: Devin-Adair, 1947.

_____. Modern Christian Revolutionaries. New York: Books for Libraries, 1971.

Beaujohn, Paul. "Eric Gill, Sculptor of Letters," The Fleuron, VIII:27-51, 1929.

Bland, David. The Illustration of Books. London: Faber and Faber, 1951.

Buhler, C. F. "Aldus Manutius, the First Five Hundred Years," Bibliographic Society of America Papers, XL: 205-215, July-Sept., 1950.

Clark Library Symposium. The Life and Works of Eric Gill. Los Angeles: University of California, 1968.

Contemporary British Artists: Eric Gill. · London: E. Benn Ltd., 1927.

DeVinne, Theodore Low. Notable Printers During the Fifteenth Century. New York: Grolier Club, 1910.

The Dolphin, Vols. I, II, and III.   New York: Limited Editions Club,   1933,   1935,   1939.

Gibbings, Robert.   "The Art of the Book,"   The Studio,
    XCVII:98-101,   Feb.,   1929.

Gill, Evan R.   Bibliography of Eric Gill.   London: Cassell
    and Company, Ltd.,   1953.

Gilson, Etienne.   Painting and Reality.   Washington, D. C.:
    Bollingen Foundation, Inc.   1957.

Goudy, Frederic.   Typologia.   Los Angeles: University of
    California Press,   1940.

Grannis, Ruth.   "Modern Fine Printing,"   The Dolphin,   III.
    New York: Limited Editions Club,   1939.

Harling, Robert.   "Type Designs of Eric Gill,"   Alphabet and
    Image,   VI:55-69,   January,   1948.

Kindersley, David.   Mr. Eric Gill: Recollections of David
    Kindersley.   San Francisco: Book Club of California,
    1967.

Jackson, Holbrook.   The Printing of Books.   London:
    Cassell and Company,   1938.

Jennett, Sean.   The Making of Books.   London: Faber and
    Faber,   1951.

Johnston, Paul.   Bibliotypographica.   New York: Covici
    Friede,   1930.

Kepes, Gyorgy, ed.   Graphic Forms: The Arts as Related
    to the Book.   Cambridge: Harvard University Press,
    1949.

_____.   The Language of Vision.   Chicago: Theobald
    Press,   1949.

Lehmann-Haupt, Helmut.   One Hundred Books About Book-
    making.   New York: Columbia University Press,   1949.

Maritain, Jacques.   Creative Intuition in Art and Poetry.
    New York: Pantheon Books,   1953.

_____. "The Secret of Beauty," Art and Faith. New
    York: Philosophical Society, 1948.

Morison, Stanley. The Typographic Arts. London: The
    Sylvan Press, 1949.

Nahm, Milton. The Artist as Creator. Baltimore: Johns
    Hopkins University Press, 1956.

Newdigate, Barnard. The Art of the Book. London: The
    Studio Limited, 1938.

Osborne, Noel, ed. The Eric Gill Memorial Collection.
    Chichester (Sussex), 1967.

Pepler, Conrad. "A Study in Integrity," Blackfriars,
    XXVIII:198-209, May, 1947.

Pepler, H. D. C. A Letter from Sussex. Chicago:
    Society of Typographic Arts, 1950.

Phelan, Gerald B. "An Artist's Philosophy," Commonweal,
    XVIII:285-286, July 14, 1933.

Phystick, J. F. The Engraved Works of Eric Gill. Lon-
    don: Victoria and Albert Museum, 1963.

Rand, Paul. Thoughts on Design. New York: Wittenborn,
    Schultz Inc. , 1947.

Rath, Erich Von. "The Spread of Printing in the Fifteenth
    Century," The Dolphin, III. New York: Limited Edi-
    tions Club, 1939.

Rogers, Bruce. Pi. Cleveland: World Publishing Com-
    pany, 1953.

Scott, Robert Gillam. Design Fundamentals. New York:
    McGraw-Hill Book Company, 1951.

Shewring, Walter. "Considerations on Eric Gill." Dublin
    Review, 1944.

Simon, Oliver and Rodenberg, Julius. Printing Today.
    London: Peter Davies Ltd. , 1928.

Speaight, Robert. The Life of Eric Gill. London: Methuen,
    1966.

Thorp, Joseph. Eric Gill. London: Jonathan Cape, 1929.

The Times Literary Supplement. London Times, 1929-1940.

Updike, Daniel Berkeley. Printing Types, Their History,
    Forms and Use: A Study in Survivals. Cambridge:
    Harvard University Press, 1922.

    _____. Some Aspects of Printing Old and New. New
    Haven: William E. Rudge, 1941.

Wroth, Lawrence, ed. "A History of the Printed Book,"
    The Dolphin, III. New York: Limited Editions Club,
    1939.

INDEX

Perpetua, 19, 20, 22, 31, 34, 35, 41, 63, 68, 75, 76-77, 79, 81, 102, 113, 114, 122

Art, 4
Art and Love, 19
Art and Prudence, 21
artist, 3
Art-Nonsense, 19, 101, 103, 115
Autobiography, 19, 99, 123

Baskerville, John, 40, 69, 122
Beauty, 4
Beauty Looks After Herself, 19, 106, 107, 112
Bembo, 24, 103
Biography, 9-17
Book design, 1, 92, 93, 94, 96, 98, 99, 103, 104, 108
Book jackets, 31, 112, 113, 116
The Book of Kells, 41, 46, 122
Bunyan (Pilgrim), 27, 34, 36, 38, 48, 49, 52, 53, 54-55, 79, 87, 88, 89, 90, 114, 115, 119, 122

Canterbury Tales, viii, 22, 23, 108, 109
Caslon, 19, 41, 122
Clark Memorial Library see William Andrews Clark Memorial Library
Clothes, 20, 99
Clothing Without Cloth, 21, 104
Colophon, 30, 33, 36
Contemporary forces, 7, 28-30, 79, 122, 123
The Constant Mistress, 22
Critics, 14, 19, 108, 111

Definitions,
    Art, 4
    Beauty, 4
    contemporary marks, 5-7
    design elements, 5
Drawings from Life, 27

Engravings, 20, 108, 124
An Essay on Typography, 28, 31, 32, 34, 65, 76-77, 113

Felicity see Perpetua and Felicity type

138

The Fleuron, 34, 35, 102, 117
The Four Gospels, 22, 26, 70, 72-73, 83, 104, 108,
        122, 123
frontispiece, 110
functional, 7, 79, 122, 123

Gill Sans, 112, 113, 116
Gill type designs see Bunyan; Gill Sans; Golden
        Cockerel; Joanna; Perpetua
Glue and Lacquer, 22, 74, 123
Golden Cockerel Press, 21
Golden Cockerel type, 22, 26, 41, 71, 72-73, 75,
        82, 83, 84, 108, 119, 122
Goudy, Fred, 114
The Green Ship, 22, 103
Greek, 56, 59, 65, 66-67, 122
Guilds, 14, 15, 16, 17, 27, 28; see also Pigotts

Hague, René, 24, 25
Hague and Gill Press, 25, 27, 28, 29, 31, 32, 33,
        34, 35, 36, 37, 60, 61, 62, 64, 65, 74, 81,
        85, 86, 88, 89, 100, 102, 105, 113; see also
        Pigotts
Hague and Gill Pressmark, 31, 113, 117
Hamlet, 30, 33, 60, 66-67, 84, 85, 100, 103, 123
The Holy Sonnets, 34, 38, 53, 88, 104

illustrations, 22, 26, 108, 109, 110, 114, 118
Incunabula, 50, 51, 58, 59
inter-linear studies,
        No. 1.   54-55   Bunyan
        No. 2.   66-67   Joanna
        No. 3.   72-73   Golden Cockerel
        No. 4.   76-77   Perpetua
international recognition, 121
italic type, 20, 35, 56, 63, 64, 68, 79, 122

Jenson, Nicolas, 42, 50, 51, 54-55
Joanna type, 28, 30, 32, 34, 37, 38, .62, 66-67, 79,
        85, 114, 119, 122
Johnson, Edward, 41

Kells   see   The Book of Kells

139

Kepes, Gyorgy, 6; The Language of Vision, 104

Lanston Monotype 34
Last days, 123-124
The Leper, The Four Gospels, 26
Letterer, 13, 16, 17, 47
Letters Drawn for Perpetua Type Design, 47
Limited Editions Club,
     Hamlet, 30, 33, 57, 60, 84, 85, 97, 100
     A Sentimental Journey, 36, 38, 52, 89
The Lord's Song, 21
The Lost Child, 27

Manuscript and Inscription Letters, 41
Manutius, Aldus, 41, 49, 56, 58, 59, 66-67, 122
Maritain, Jacque, The Responsibility of the Artist,
     124
marriage, 13
minuscules, The Book of Kells, 40
Money and Morals, 28

new forms see Gill type designs
Notes, The Aldine Bible, 64

Pannartz see Sweynheim and Pannartz
paper, 98-99, 103
paperbacks see pocketbooks
Passio Domini, 104, 118
The Passion of Our Lord, 34
The Passion of Perpetua and Felicity, 29, 34, 35,
     76-77, 81, 102, 104, 122
The Penrose Annual, 119
Perpetua type, 19, 20, 22, 34, 41, 63, 79, 114, 119
Phaedo, 103
Pigotts, 16, 24, 25, 27-28, 56, 57, 63, 84
Pilgrim see Bunyan type
Plates,
     Aldine Bible, 61, 64, 66-67, 110
     Art-Nonsense, 101, 115
     John Baskerville, 69
     Beauty Looks After Herself, 106, 107, 112
     The Book of Kells, 46
     Canterbury Tales, viii, 23, 109

140

DATE DUE